A Place We Call Home

Syracuse Studies on Peace and Conflict Resolution
Robert A. Rubenstein, *Series Editor*

A Place We Call
HOME

GENDER, RACE, AND JUSTICE IN SYRACUSE

K. Animashaun Ducre

SYRACUSE UNIVERSITY PRESS

∞ The paper used in this publication meets the minimum requirements of the American
National Standard for Information Sciences—Permanence of Paper for Printed Library
Materials, ANSI Z39.48-1992.

For a listing of books published and distributed by Syracuse University Press,
visit our website at SyracuseUniversityPress.syr.edu.

ISBN: 978-0-8156-3306-8

Library of Congress Cataloging-in-Publication Data
Ducre, K. Animashaun.
A place we call home : gender, race, and justice in Syracuse /
K. Animashaun Ducre. — 1st ed.
p. cm.
Includes bibliographical references and index.
ISBN 978-0-8156-3306-8 (cloth : alk. paper) 1. African American neighborhoods—
New York (State)—Syracuse. 2. African American mothers—New York
(State)—Syracuse—Social conditions. 3. Community life—New York (State)—
Syracuse. 4. Environmental justice—New York (State)—Syracuse.
5. Feminist theory. I. Title.
HN80.S94D83 2012
305.896074766—dc23   2012040260

Manufactured in the United States of America

K. Animashaun Ducre is assistant professor in the Department of African American Studies at Syracuse University. She received her PhD in the Environmental Justice Program of the University of Michigan's School of Natural Resources and Environment in 2005.

Kishi has been a committed advocate for environmental justice for more than a decade. Her first foray in environmental activism was as a Toxics Campaigner for Greenpeace from 1994 to 1997. She combines her experiences on the frontlines of the environmental justice movement and academic training in geographic information systems and demography for a unique perspective on economic and environmental inequality in the United States.

Contents

Illustrations

Acknowledgments

Funding for this project was made possible through a grant from the Ford Foundation and a subvention grant from Dean George Langford of the College of Arts and Sciences at Syracuse University. I would also like to thank my colleagues in the Department of African American Studies, Sandra Lane in the Falk College of Human and Sport Dynamics, and Michael Spencer from the School of Social Work at the University of Michigan. I am also grateful for the research assistance and amazing transcription from Ingrid Butler, PhD candidate in the Department of Geography. I'd also like to thank Kheli Willetts and Gina Cooke at the Community Folk Art Center for help in producing the community Photovoice exhibition and Jonnell Allen Robinson, the Syracuse Community Geographer who provided the maps for this project.

My gratitude is also extended to the work and mission of the Syracuse Community Health Center and other community health centers who assist the underserved all across this nation. Of course this project would not be possible without the time, attention, and steadfast commitment from the women who participated in the project.

I'd also like to thank the anonymous reviewers for their input on earlier versions of the manuscript and the not-so-anonymous reviews by Sabrina Denham Rogers and Stephanie Hatch Richards. Kudos to the great staff at Syracuse University Press.

And Brad, thanks for all you do!

Abbreviations

CANT	Citizens Against Nuclear Trash
CBPAR	community-based participatory action research
CORE	Congress of Racial Equality
CSO	combined sewer overflows
GAO	General Accounting Office
GED	General Education Diploma
HOLC	Home Owners' Loan Corporation
IES	Impact of Events Scale
POC	Partnership for Onondaga Creek
SAEJ	Southeast Alliance for Environmental Justice
SES	socioeconomic status
SFE	San Francisco Energy
UCC	United Church of Christ

A Place We Call Home

An Introduction

There are a few Simple Truths that we still believe in:

Every species has the right to clean air, clean water, clean soil, and an unthreatened existence. For over twenty years, whenever any of these environmental rights has been violated, we have called attention to this injustice by speaking out and, when necessary, by using direct action and dramatic images, bearing witness for the Earth.

—1994 Woodstock Greenpeace Staff T-shirt

I worked for Greenpeace from 1993 to 1997. Its mission statement continues to reflect my own life's work of bearing witness to social injustice. One of the benefits of working for Greenpeace was that you acquire a number of T-shirts. Greenpeace protests are carefully organized spectacles, and all participants typically wear the same uniform: a T-shirt depicting the action in a visually arresting graphic with a sound bite–sized slogan.

I still have my collection of Greenpeace T-shirts. One of my favorites comes from a World Bank protest in Washington, D.C. The shirt depicts the classic Frankenstein character, except his name is World Bankenstein. With the words "No Dollars for Destruction" emblazoned in green across the top, this organic cotton T-shirt shows the evil Bankenstein clutching a chainsaw above an industrial area with belching smokestacks. In the foreground, there's a forest ravaged by clearcutting. Another T-shirt bears the opening quote for this chapter. It was worn by the Greenpeace staffers who worked at the 1994 concert commemorating Woodstock in upstate New York. My primary task during the three-day festival focused on giving tours of Cyrus, Greenpeace's mobile, solar-powered generator. The Woodstock experience left a lot to be desired: the rain, the mud, the frustration of attempting to promote clean energy among stoned concertgoers. At least I got a free T-shirt.

For those activists who work for environmental causes along with other social justice issues, the concept of bearing witness means advocating on behalf of those who can't advocate for themselves. Sometimes the task is to speak for these marginalized voices. Or sometimes bearing witness means amplifying their voices. In fact, my early activist work reflected the politics of each era. In Washington, D.C., during the 1980s, Mitch Snyder and the Community for Creative Non-Violence pressed the plight of the homeless. Consequently, my family and I worked in food kitchens and gave out baskets to the needy. The adults drove around on cold nights to distribute blankets. In college during the early 1990s, my activism shifted to focus on issues of racial intolerance. During my first year at Tulane University, some African American freshmen were targeted with anonymous racial hate mail. The Rodney King beating in 1991, the subsequent acquittal of the officers involved, and the explosive riots in Los Angeles also had a profound impact on my political development. It was not until I joined Greenpeace in 1994 that I became an advocate within the environmental justice movement.

Environmental racism is the pattern of locating unwanted land uses in and around communities of color and poor neighborhoods. In the 1990s the environmental justice movement was very successful in raising the level of national awareness of environmental inequality. The First National People of Color Environmental Leadership Summit was held in Washington, D.C., in 1991, and environmental racism became a national rallying cry of communities of color and poor neighborhoods that were slated for new projects that involved potentially harmful chemical processing and storage. More than five hundred activists attended the summit, where they created and adopted the seventeen Principles of Environmental Justice. The movement reached its zenith in 1994 when President Clinton signed an Executive Order on Environmental Justice. This order formally recognized the efforts of the environmental justice movement and ordered federal agencies to review their policies to insure equal protection. Efforts to create a federal environmental justice law have since been attempted, but as of this writing none has succeeded.

In 1996, I became an integral part of the campaign to stop Shintech, a Japanese plastics company, from building its latest chemical manufacturing complex that produced the feedstocks for creating polyvinyl chloride plastics in the small town of Convent, Louisiana. This was a precedent-setting battle for the environmental justice movement and served as another instance of my quest to bear witness. Ultimately the opponents of the Shintech project were successful. But on a personal level I faced burnout after a protracted and relentless struggle to protect communities against chemical projects. I turned my energies from bearing witness on the frontlines of the fight for environmental justice in order to pursue an academic career. I continued my environmental justice advocacy within academia.

The early research efforts on environmental racism and injustice occurred in the 1980s: the 1983 study by the Federal General Accounting Office (GAO) and the 1987 study by the Commission for Racial Justice of the United Church of Christ (UCC). The GAO report was one of the first major studies to examine the racial and economic characteristics of neighborhoods that host hazardous waste facilities. A few years later, the Commission for Racial Justice expanded on the GAO report to a national analysis of the relationship between race, class, and environmental exposure. Both studies concluded that people of color and the poor were more likely to reside near hazardous waste facilities.

Environmental justice scholarship has centered primarily on measuring the disproportionate impacts on these overburdened communities (Evans and Kantrowitz 2002; Liu 2001; Maantay 2002; Pulido 1996; Szasz and Meuser 1997). Much of the analysis focuses on racial and class inequalities. There has been very little research on gender (Brown and Ferguson 1995; DiChiro 1999; Klawiter 1999) or on the multiplicative effects of race, class, and gender. I believe this scholarship would greatly benefit from the theoretical contributions of feminism and spatiality.

The purpose of this book is to build a bridge between Black feminist theory and environmental justice scholarship through the words, images, and spatial imaginings of African American mothers in the South Side of Syracuse. More specifically, my intent is to explain the lived experiences of African American mothers in an impoverished neighborhood within the city of Syracuse and how they respond to the built environment. I will describe how these women manage their daily survival in these degraded environments, the tools that they deploy to do so, and how they act as agents of change in their communities. To this end, my task is not only to point out the structural obstacles of living, working, and playing in an area plagued with environmental neglect but also to highlight the strength and agency of those women, who manage to prosper in the face of such obstacles.

Making the Case for Gender in Environmental Justice

At the heart of most feminist scholarship is the act of bearing witness. Feminist theorists acknowledge the marginality or outright invisibility of women's voices in academic research and methods. They have introduced the notion of a gendered way of knowing and of a feminist epistemology. What does it mean to employ a Black feminist epistemological approach? It means that this project places Black women's experiences at the center of analysis (Collins 1990). My methodology highlights the interlocking systems of oppression that Black women must face as a consequence of their race, class standing, and gender. Undertaking a Black feminist epistemological approach has two functions. First, it challenges conventional ideas that seek to essentialize poor Black women's oppression in purely racial, class, or gendered terms. Patricia Hill Collins refers to this practice as "the politics of containment" (1998, 35). Second, this approach is committed to the notion of Black women as agents of social change.

My work relies on two critical elements within Black feminist epistemology: intersectionality and the personal narrative. As Dill and Zambrana note, intersectionality deals with the "complexity rather than the singular of human experience" (2009, 2). It recognizes that individuals can occupy multiple social locations and expands on conventional feminism that essentialized women. The use of an intersectional frame seems to be a natural fit in environmental justice scholarship. After all, environmental justice literature focuses on how environmental assets and deficits are unequally distributed, primarily based on one's race and class location. However, the earliest scholarship on environmental justice created a false dichotomy, because it debated whether environmental inequalities were based more on race or on class. Geographer Laura Pulido (1996) has been a vocal critic of the methodology of conventional environmental justice research, particularly when it comes to scholars' treatment of race and class variables. She calls the tendency to create a race and class dichotomy in environmental justice scholarship a trap. An intersectionality frame circumvents the tendency to compare the disadvantages posed by race with those posed by class. Instead, it opens the analysis to understanding the ways in which race, class, gender, and other forms of marginalized identities affect how environmental burdens and benefits are distributed. The intersectional frame does not engage in questions of which marginalized status is worse but seeks to add complexity and dimension to the notion of multiple oppressions.

The second critical element of undertaking a Black feminist approach is the reliance upon personal narrative. Essential to her critique of what she called bourgeois (white) feminism, bell hooks recalls her experience as a graduate student in a feminist theory course in 1981. She was affronted by the total absence of readings by women of color and was vocal in her critique. She was met with derision. "When I suggested that the purpose of this collective anger was to create an atmosphere in which it would be psychologically unbearable for me to speak in class discussions or even attend class, I was told that they were not angry. *I* was the one who was angry" (hooks 1995, 280). Likewise, Audre Lorde shares her experience as a lesbian of color within the larger feminist movement: "As a forty-nine-year-old Black lesbian feminist socialist mother of two including one boy, and a member of an interracial couple, I usually find myself a part of some group defined as other, deviant, inferior, or just plain wrong" (1995, 284). Lorde's words seem to throw off the cloak of oppression and invisibility experienced by women of color. The use of personal experience runs counter to social science, whose foundation on ostensible objectivity eschews any personal inclination or *bias*. The founders of modern social science were adamant in their call for a divide between the personal and the political to maintain objectivity in research. In fact, the roots of sociology rest on the principle of value-free scholarship. Incorporating personal narrative into a research project challenges this personal-objective divide. This deviation is validated by the use of feminist epistemology and centers on a gendered (and raced) way of knowing that privileges marginalized voices. My project follows those tenets of feminist epistemology. Within the women's stories of hope, survival, and identity that follow, I also find my own story. Most chapters connect my story to the narrative of the overall project. Therefore this book not only presents the testimonies of some Black mothers in Syracuse but also bears witness to my own personal journey from the daughter of a struggling single mom in Southeast Washington, D.C., to a Greenpeace hellraiser, to college professor and environmental justice scholar.

Making the Case for Space in Environmental Justice

In her book *Left of Karl Marx*, Carol Boyce Davies points out the lack of a geopolitical framework within U.S. Black feminist literature. For Davies, U.S. Black feminists fail to place themselves within the context of imperialism, critical in regards to transnational feminism. Under transnational feminism, gender oppression is grounded within a historical, political, and spatial context. She writes: "most critical in doing transnational feminist work is the understanding that the nation-states in which we live as subjects have been produced out of specific political imperatives and history and that they seek to contain, arbitrarily, a variety of peoples subject to the whims of these nation-states enterprises" (2007, 21). She critiques early Black feminist work for its failure to acknowledge U.S. imperialism: "If those nation-states attain dominance, as has happened in the case of the United States, then even those identities subordinated domestically in those states are unwittingly attached" (2007, 21). Although I appreciate the challenges that Davies highlights, her charges appear reductionist. There is a tradeoff when choosing to link Diasporic and Third World feminisms within a geopolitical frame, thereby suggesting a relative advantage for women of color who reside in rich nation-states. A transnational feminist might suggest that being a poor Black woman in the United States may be qualitatively different in material circumstances from being a poor Black woman in Haiti. However, witnessing the impact of Hurricane Katrina on poor Black women in New Orleans tells us that they share more with their sisters in the developing world than we may have previously been able to comprehend. What I find most useful in Davies' critique is the idea of spatiality. In this instance, spatiality refers how gender oppression operates given its regional or geopolitical context. I propose that the association between U.S. Black feminism and transnational feminism converge on the concept of spatiality, particularly within an environmental justice frame.

After all, spatiality is a primary component in environmental justice theorizing. Dialogue centers on the *location* of a hazardous industry in relation to communities of color and poor neighborhoods. Researchers have sought to investigate environmental racism and injustice by measuring the degree to which hazardous industries are located near marginalized peoples through the use of elaborate spatial modeling techniques. Despite strides in these spatial measures and modeling, there are to date relatively few works on spatial theorizing in environmental justice. Again, Pulido has been critical of the literature's treatment of racism as a discrete act rather than as a social-spatial process (Pulido 2000; Pulido et al. 1996). My previous work attempted to address this gap in spatial theorizing in environmental justice through a concept I refer to as *racialized space*. I define racialized space as the historic practice and spatial designation of a particular area for racial and ethnic minorities as a means of containment and social control. My racialized space hypothesis is largely a structural analysis of environmental racism. It focuses on how the policies of social institutions like the government, law enforcement, and the housing finance industry prohibit the physical and social mobility of the poor and communities of color. This book moves from the broader structural issues related to racialized space to include a focus on agency. *Agency* is a sociological concept that refers to the power and autonomy of social actors to think and behave beyond structural constraints. More specifically, this current investigation builds upon Black feminist theory by exploring Black women's agency and resistance to racialized space.

My task in this book is not to speak for these African American mothers. My task is to amplify and shine light on their lives and experiences, focusing on the ways in which race, gender, and space intersect. To do this, I employ two research methodologies: community mapping and Photovoice.

Community mapping is a broad term to describe a process in which individual stakeholders come together to create a visual image of their environment, highlighting its assets and deficiencies. The group must reach consensus on the boundaries of the said environment (*what consti-tutes our community*) and agree upon the variables by which the environ-ment is mapped (*what constitutes green space, blight, good areas, problem areas, etc.*). Community mapping has been a tool in urban planning, crime prevention, resource management, health promotion, and asset-mapping. I borrow this method from the doctoral work of Cheryl Teelucksingh (2001; 2002), who relied on data from participatory mapping exercises with resi-dents from three communities in Toronto, Ontario, Canada. The South Side mothers were given maps of their neighborhood to determine the extent of their spatiality and to establish their interpretation of positive versus negative spaces.

Photovoice is an innovative participatory research strategy that began in the field of public health and health promotion (Wang et al. 1998). The first use of this methodology was by women in rural China (Wang and Bur-ris 1994). It has been described as a process that "aims to use photographic images taken by persons with little money, power, or status to enhance community needs assessments, empower participants and induce change by informing policy makers of community assets and deficits" (Strack et al. 2004, 49). Photovoice participants are typically the most marginalized in a society. Projects have included images produced from youth in Flint, Mich-igan (Hwang 1999; Wang and Redwood-Jones 2001), Baltimore, Maryland (Strack et al. 2004), and West Contra Costa County, California (Wilson et al. 2006); KwaZulu-Natal (Zulu Kingdom) in South Africa (International Visual Methodologies for Social Change Project n.d.); homeless shelter residents in Ann Arbor, Michigan (Wang et al. 2000); and elderly and homeless African American women (Killion and Wang 2000).

The Photovoice process typically involves a series of workshops where participants learn the basics of photography and discuss issues related to their community. Next, participants go into their community to capture images of their neighborhoods. In subsequent sessions, participants select their best images, write captions, and participate in a facilitated discussion. Most Photovoice projects end with a community exhibition, during which invited community leaders and policymakers have a critical dialogue with Photovoice participants. The South Side moms I worked with engaged in similar Photovoice sessions and hosted a community exhibition at the end of the project. This book will present key themes in their images and compare and contrast those themes with past Photovoice projects.

Thus, *A Place We Call Home* chronicles the role of race, gender, environmental justice, and space in the city of Syracuse. It does so in three specific thrusts: The first goal is to bear witness to environmental injustice and structural relations of power and space. The second but central task involves bearing witness to Black women's agency when dealing with structural obstacles: how do these women maintain dignity and restore order in an environment in which they have historically had very little control? What constitutes safety, stability, and goodness? What constitutes risk or danger and how do they avoid it? Finally, the evaluative element of this project is my assessment of how this process of bearing witness serves as a useful methodology in feminist research.

Chapter 2 introduces the demographics of the South Side community as well as the fourteen women who agreed to go on this journey. Josephine, Billie, Nikki, Makeba, CJ, Faith, Gwen, Elizabeth, Barbara, Nina, Shirley, Katherine, Zora, and Harriet all agreed to take a month-long workshop, using maps and pictures to describe their neighborhood and their experiences. I am the fifteenth participant, and this chapter also highlights aspects of my own life in the context of the other participants' experiences. I introduce readers to my grandmother, and how working with the South Side women reawakened memories of her dignity amid structural oppression.

Chapter 3 chronicles the persistent cycles of disruption and dislocation of the African American community in Syracuse. The critical assumption in this chapter is that the South Side neighborhood became a racialized space. The city of Syracuse and its neighboring communities fostered city and regional development at the expense of the African American community's access to affordable, safe, and clean housing. Key moments focus on the first Black city dwellers, the impact of redlining, and the city's urban renewal project, including the construction of highway I-81. In critically accounting for racialized space within Syracuse, I rely on historical city planning maps.

Chapter 4 features the results of the community mapping exercise. The key questions to be answered are (1) what constitutes the areas that are labeled "good"? (2) what constitutes areas that are labeled "bad"?, and (3) what are the patterns of similarity/dissimilarity among the participants' maps?

Chapter 5 presents the main themes that emerged from the Photovoice workshops and the community exhibition that followed. These results are particularly revealing when situated against other Photovoice projects, primarily those with mothers and African American women as participants. I also discuss my own transformation as a result of the project.

Finally, chapter 6 evaluates the strength of the project in its claims about spatiality and gender in environmental justice scholarship. I believe that community mapping and Photovoice are useful in feminist research and I discuss the implications of the work in the future.

2

Welcome to the South Side

At a recent reception held in a faculty member's home, tucked into the quietly prosperous university neighborhood, I found myself standing among a group of other professors lamenting the difficult academic life while eating catered Indian food. *I am just so busy. It's hard for me to find time to write. Grading is so time-consuming.* I joined in for a while. I was busy and I wasn't able to write as much as I thought I would after my life as a graduate student. And, yes, grading during midterms and finals can cause one's eyes to water. But really, was my life particularly tough?

During this classic faculty whining session, I felt a cosmic kick to my temple. I had an involuntary physical response to the idea that in the middle of a workday afternoon, I had the privilege of standing around in someone's home, eating catered food, and complaining about how difficult things were for me. I was suddenly aware of how spoiled I sounded. Later, I recalled that moment as an epiphany around the memory of Nana, my grandmother, who passed away in 2000.

Nana, or Louise Pettus, came into the world on August 16, 1930. She was the fifth of eight children born to Earline Smith from Winston-Salem, North Carolina. Like many African American families during the early twentieth century, the Smiths escaped Southern poverty in search of better economic opportunity in the North. The family first arrived in Harlem, New York, where Louise and two of her younger siblings were born. They eventually settled in the southeast section of the highly segregated city of Washington, DC. Nana graduated from high school, had three children, and spent the majority of her life raising them as a single mom. She earned a living by working in a uniform cleaning plant for nearly thirty years. For decades, Nana spent each day taking laundered uniforms out of a chemical bath and steaming them until they were fresh and crisp. I think of that back-breaking labor in awe: thirty years of standing up and ironing.

I was Nana's first grandchild, and now I was lamenting about how tough I had it? That afternoon I took stock and acknowledged how far I had come from my grandmother's life. She was an undereducated domestic worker, and I am a professor at a private university. Years of education have catapulted me from that very same house where Nana lived in Southeast DC into the cushy confines of a university neighborhood. The transition from that space that I used to occupy into the one I currently find myself is quite an amazing journey. I thought of Nana again when I stood before a group of Black women in the summer of 2007. I had just begun a series of workshops to explore how Black women navigate in oppressive spaces. That same quiet dignity that Nana had in the face of the harsh realities of structural oppression—racial segregation, economic deprivation, and limited resources—was echoed in the faces of the women in my research project.

It was Saturday morning, June 9, 2007, and I was in the multipurpose room of the local health clinic awaiting women who signed up to participate in the Syracuse Community Mapping and Health Photovoice Project. My colleague and I were the recipients of a Ford Foundation grant, and the project was research supported by those funds. I was quite nervous, despite the fact that I have been organizing community workshops for years. Three months after graduating from Tulane University in New Orleans in 1993, I took a job as a campaigner for Greenpeace, an international environmental organization, at its headquarters in Washington, D.C. Less than a month later, I was sent to help organize a protest at the Masters Golf Invitational in Augusta, Georgia. Residents of Hyde Park and Aragon Park in Augusta vowed to fight against the environmental contamination in their neighborhoods. Years of processing at a wood treatment plant and a scrap metal facility left soil and air contaminants like lead, arsenic, and PCBs. After that beginning in Augusta, I spent the next four years mobilizing similar community groups, primarily in California and Louisiana.

But that day in June 2007, I was more nervous than I'd ever been as a Greenpeace campaigner. My new role was as a scholar, not just as an activist. I had recently completed the second year of my tenure-track position at Syracuse University's Department of African American Studies. Earlier that year, a colleague and I had been awarded that grant to highlight the intersection of Black Feminism and Environmental Justice in our department's curriculum. I convinced my colleague and representatives at the local public health service that this mapping and photography project was an ideal vehicle to explore issues related to women and the environment. That morning, it felt like the stakes were much higher. It was an ambitious project, consisting of five events: four consecutive Saturday workshops and an exhibition at a local art gallery. The first workshop would cover community mapping. For the second workshop, the participants would come to campus for photography lessons and tour a photography laboratory. The final two workshops would focus on the Photovoice results, where participants would present their photos and discuss ideas about their community.

The South Side community was a natural selection for this project. It sits right near the Syracuse University campus but is starkly separated by racial and economic privilege. Syracuse's South Side includes census tracts 42, 52, 53, 54, and 58. The tracts represented populations as small as 1,895 to 3,230. About four out of every five residents in this area are African American. Nearly half of all households were headed by single mothers. In 1999 in most of these census tracts nearly one quarter of all households subsisted on a median income of less than $10,000. Residents within census tract 42 were worse off than the rest, with more than half of the households earning less than $10,000.

In the weeks prior to the workshop, volunteers at the local public health facility recruited female clients. Participants were eligible to join the project if they met five criteria: they had to identify as an African American woman, be over the age of eighteen, live with at least one child or grandchild under eighteen, have lived in the South Side for at least five years, and be willing to attend the Saturday workshops. For their participation, each woman would receive $40 in cash per Saturday workshop along with a digital camera, camera bag, memory card, and rechargeable batteries. The volunteers recruited thirty-four women in all. Five of those who were interested proved ineligible. Out of the remaining pool of potential participants, fifteen names were randomly drawn; twelve as participants and three as alternates. In the end, fourteen participants completed the project. Amazingly, there was zero percent participation attrition. While some may have missed a workshop, all of the women completed the project and submitted images to the community exhibition at its conclusion.

The average age of the participants was thirty-seven, with the youngest being twenty-one and the oldest forty-four. Their average number of children was three. Four participants had only one child, and one reported having six children at home. The average length of time that participants had resided on the South Side was fourteen years, with the shortest time being five years and the longest being over thirty-four years. The names of the participants have been changed to ensure confidentiality and anonymity. To honor these women, I assigned each a pseudonym from an African American female icon: *Josephine, Billie, Nikki, Makeba, CJ, Faith, Gwen, Elizabeth, Barbara, Nina, Shirley, Katherine, Zora,* and *Harriet.*

Josephine was very enthusiastic about the project. I assigned her the name Josephine as homage to the late Josephine Baker, an entertainer in the 1920s and American expatriate to France. While Baker the icon has often been unfairly reduced to depictions of her provocative performances, I was struck by her fierce independence and courage to forge her own destiny in a time when there were few opportunities for Black women. Josephine the participant had lived in the South Side for most of her adult life. Her coloring was dramatic; she had a light complexion, reddish-blonde hair, and an easy smile. She lived in a home with three children and spoke of her son quite often over the course of the workshop. She was particularly proud of his accomplishments as an athlete and as a student.

It was easy to come up with the namesake for the next participant, *Billie*. Like the original Billie Holiday, Billie was a contradiction of toughness from a hard life battling drug addiction and grace in her speech and thoughtfulness. She was of medium height, thin with a dark complexion. She seemed to be aware of all of the simultaneous conversations among the mothers in the room and was knowledgeable about the South Side's geography. Billie was the heartbeat of the group in many ways, very lively in discussions and painfully honest about her life. I was amazed at her candor. Billie was held in such regard that she was nominated by the other members to speak at the community exhibition at the end of the project. She had lived in Syracuse for eight years and resided with one child.

The participants seemed to divide into two groups in age and life experience. There was a relatively young group of four participants in their early twenties, three of whom had toddlers. One of the young members of the group I named *Nikki,* for the poet Nikki Giovanni. She always came to the workshops dressed in a masculine style, with a hat pulled low on her forehead, boxy shirts, and loose-fitting pants. Unlike Billie, she was not as forthcoming about her life. Nikki had the cutest toddler, whom she photographed frequently with her new digital camera. She had lived in the South Side for five years.

Makeba was another young mother, who had lived in the South Side for six years. I gave her the name of the late South African singer and activist, Miriam Makeba. Like most of the younger mothers, Makeba's dress and hairstyle were casual. She also had a toddler that she brought to one of the sessions. Makeba's little girl, just learning to walk, was crawling everywhere. That day, Makeba's burden of stress as a young mother was eased, because without conscious thought or discussion the women took turns engaging the precocious toddler. This communal mothering is a hallmark of the Black community. Makeba was probably the youngest of the group and was extremely shy when addressing them as a whole. When I spoke with her one-on-one before and after the workshops, she became much more relaxed. She was also enthusiastic about the project and really enjoyed the group's visit to the campus photography lab. After receiving her digital camera, Makeba returned to the following week's session with over a hundred photos.

CJ is named for the late, great Madame CJ Walker, one of the first Black millionaires, who built her empire on hair and beauty products. True to her name designation, CJ displayed her flair as the most well-dressed and well-coiffed of the group. Originally an alternate, CJ was called into the project a week after it began and was thrilled to be able to join. She was in her late forties, both a mother with children living at home and a grandmother who lived in the South Side for ten years. During one Photovoice session, she presented a photo of a public bus; she complained of riding the city bus because she was unable to afford car repairs. Despite her limited funds, CJ always appeared picture perfect: her dark brown hair was smoothed into a ponytail of silky weave. Her outfits were well-coordinated, down to the color-matched heels.

After I complimented Josephine on her shoes one Saturday, some of the participants encouraged me to go to AJ Wright, a discount department store in a strip mall called Shop City. When I wondered aloud about the location of Shop City, they were aghast, further cementing my outsider status. *How could I not know the location of Shop City?* I think they were amused and oddly comforted by my flashes of confusion throughout the course of the project, because it demonstrated that there was much I could learn from them. I was well aware of the range of possibilities of how the group might perceive me. On the one hand, I looked like them: I was the same race and within the same age range. I believe that those similarities may have helped them to trust me. On the other hand, I came from outside the South Side and was a representative of Syracuse University, euphemistically known among locals as "the Hill," reflecting historic tensions between the university and the local community. Ironically, I don't think they understood that I was a professor during that first meeting, most likely due to my relative youth.

If the project could be said to have a success story, it would be *Faith*. Her namesake is the artist Faith Ringgold, who awes art lovers with her incredible quilts and other fabric art. Like the artist, Faith's deep creativity came out in her photography. One of Faith's photos was featured in a public address given by Syracuse University Chancellor Nancy Cantor later that year. Faith was petite, a young mother of one child who had lived in the South Side for seven years. She had called me prior to the first workshop, quite upset that her GED exam was scheduled for the same time. She seemed to be considering postponing the exam in favor of the project. I convinced her to take the exam and come late. Two weeks later, Faith brought her exam results to share the good news with everyone that she had passed.

Gwen, another of the group's young mothers, was a reference to the late poet Gwendolyn Brooks. Gwen the participant was pretty quiet, as if she chose each word carefully. She was intense and earnest in her participation. She reminded me of the poet in her quiet intellect. At the project's first session, she was near the end of a pregnancy. During our break for lunch, she told me that her baby's due date was the following Wednesday and assured me that she would still try to make it to our next meeting. I quipped that if she hadn't delivered by the following Saturday's session, we were so close to the hospital that it wouldn't be a problem—spoken like a woman who had never given birth. Gwen did deliver a little boy that week and, true to her word, came to the next Saturday session with him, only a few days old, along with her other child. I was humbled by her level of commitment.

Two participants, *Elizabeth* and *Barbara,* seemed to be close friends. Elizabeth had lived on the South Side all of her life and had four children at home. Her pseudonym was inspired by the sculptor and graphic artist, Elizabeth Catlett. Like Faith, the participant Elizabeth's photography demonstrated levels of complexity. Despite the fact that she didn't talk very much, her pictures delved into issues of spirituality, peace, and absent fathers. I named her friend in honor of Barbara Jordan, who in 1972 became the first African American woman to represent a Southern state in the U.S. House of Representatives. Unfortunately, I never got a real sense of Barbara the participant. She missed half of the sessions. Like Gwen, she was expecting a baby and through snatches of her informal conversation with other women in the room, I understood that she also had experienced drug addiction. She had lived on the South Side for seven years and had six children.

Nina was one of the older mothers, with four children at home, the youngest being a toddler. She had lived in the South Side for fifteen years, and had recently experienced the murder of a close relative. Nina was named in honor of the late folk singer, Nina Simone, who gifted us with songs like "Mississippi Goddamn" to rail at the injustice in the South of the 1960s. I remember being struck by the sadness in Nina's eyes upon our first meeting. However, her demeanor was not at all sad; she was quick to laugh at the antics of the other members of the group.

Like her namesake, Shirley Chisholm, who in 1972 was the first African American *and* the first woman to run for president, *Shirley* was the most outspoken among the group. She was so opinionated that she sometimes came across as a bully. Like the others, Shirley was candid about her life and honest about the difficulties she overcame as a recovering drug addict. She made no excuses. What I found intriguing about Shirley was her level of social conservatism. Despite her difficult past, she was decidedly unsympathetic to individuals who made poor life choices. She dogmatically insisted on personal accountability. She had lived in the South Side for more than twenty years and was a grandmother.

Katherine, an older mother, was more vocal than most. If Billie was the group's cheerleader, then Katherine was its security officer. She seemed to be acquainted with some of the women in the group, and when Shirley crossed the boundaries of civility she was the one who confronted her, albeit diplomatically. Katherine is named in honor of the late Katherine Dunham, a renowned dancer. Katherine the participant lived with two children and had been a resident of the South Side for five years. Like Barbara, Billie, and Shirley, she spoke openly of her history with drug addiction.

Zora is named for one of my favorite Black icons: Zora Neale Hurston, a folk historian, anthropologist, and writer of such classics as *Their Eyes Are Watching God.* Zora was quite a character. She usually came to the workshops wearing sunglasses, which she kept on throughout the session. She wore her hair in an atypical, bleached short haircut. She was enthusiastic and engaged throughout the project. I had the nagging sense that Zora came to some of the workshops under the influence of something but was never able to confirm it. The week after I gave everyone their digital cameras, Zora called my cell phone to tell me that she had dropped her camera while she was on her bike and a car ran over it. From then on, we developed Zora's pictures from a disposable camera. Zora the participant was as colorful as Hurston, her namesake. She had lived in the South Side her entire life and lived in a home with three children.

Last but not least was the participant named in honor of Harriet Tubman, a true heroine with the strength, courage, and fortitude to lead over three hundred slaves to freedom. *Harriet* the participant was one of the older women of the group, steadfast and religious. She had lived in the South Side for nine years and lived with two children. Unlike the others, her photography depicted the more positive aspects of her community; even she was surprised by the optimism and happiness in her work. She remarked during the exhibition that by photographing her community she had gained a more positive view of it. Harriet and her camera looked beyond the landscape of urban decay to find neighbors with meticulous gardens and notable institutions like area churches and schools.

Despite my lack of knowledge of Syracuse geography (especially the location of Shop City), I shared some social attributes with the women in this project and with the residents of the South Side. I did not have children, but I was just beginning to think about starting a family. I had lived in Syracuse for only two years, but I grew up in neighborhoods very similar to the demographics of the South Side. My first recollection of home was Nana's house at 5029 A Street in Southeast D.C. Both Nana and my widowed great-grandmother Ma Smith lived there. I can recall the layout most vividly. In my childhood memory it seemed an immense house. The outside stone was painted white with a garish, hand-painted bright red trim. From its front door, you could see straight back, shotgun style, into the kitchen, the last room in the house. The first room on the right from the main door was Ma Smith's room and the next room on the right belonged to Nana. The rooms on the left of the main hallway were the living room and the dining room. The living room was decorated in 1970s style gold lamé and velvet burnout wallpaper. The dining room was where Ma Smith spent most of her time. Both my great-grandmother and grandmother kept me while my mother, a single parent, took college courses part time and went to work. The rest of my adolescence is a blur of apartments and rental homes in predominantly Black and low-income neighborhoods in Washington, D.C., and Prince George's County, Maryland. My mother and I never lived anywhere longer than a year or two. There were the urine-smelling hallways of the Belle Park apartments. I recall a rental home in Palmer Park, Maryland, when I was in middle school. I vaguely remember living in an apartment off Brightseat Road in Landover, Maryland; my sole recollection of that residence is being evicted, with our belongings being tossed out and littering the entrance of the complex. I recall feeling complete devastation, looking at my mother's black-and-white couch and other pieces of our lives sitting on the curb. Our second home in the Palmer Park neighborhood was one that my mother tried to buy but eventually lost in foreclosure. I can also recall another apartment on Georgia Avenue in

D.C. where I lived with my mother and her second husband. It was down the street from a strip club called the Foxy Playground, a fascinating term for a ten-year-old.

By the time I reached high school, I simply kept most of my stuff in boxes. I didn't unpack all of my boxes until I was living on my own during my first year on the job for Greenpeace. Unpacking was a major milestone for me; it signaled the establishment of roots. It was not until I moved into my current home in Syracuse that I not only unpacked but also discarded my boxes for the first time. By the time I began to write about the Syracuse Community Mapping and Health Photovoice project, I'd lived in my current home in Syracuse for four years, the longest that I've stayed in one place in my entire life. I've come a long way.

The Long, Hot Summer

Outside the building where the project participants and I gathered that summer, Syracuse South Side was experiencing one of its most violent summers ever. During that one-month period, the local daily newspaper reported eleven separate shootings on the South Side, along with six stabbings. These incidents resulted in three deaths. Most of the victims were young Black men between the ages of fifteen and twenty-five. One of the stabbing deaths hit close to home: On the night after our third workshop, Sunday, June 17, a fight broke out between two patrons at a bar on South Salina Street, close to Shirley and Nina's homes. The fight ended in the murder of a thirty-eight-year-old man in the bar parking lot. His death was Syracuse's eighth homicide that summer. Within that same week, the South Side would be stunned by escalating friction at an annual community event, the Juneteenth Celebration.

One of the most eagerly awaited events during the summer is the Juneteenth Celebration: a citywide recognition of African American history and culture. In Syracuse, the weekend festival in June commemorates the announcement of the end of slavery in Texas. While Lincoln's Emancipation Proclamation was enacted on September 22, 1862, it was not until June 19, 1865, that Texas slaves were told that they were free, after Union troops invaded Galveston, Texas, and enforced Lincoln's proclamation. Thus, the term, Juneteenth signifies "June 19th" and the bitter memory that slaves were not freed until nearly three years after they were duly emancipated. The South Side community and many of its leaders are the unofficial hosts and sponsors of the city's celebration. On Thursday, June 16, 2007, the celebration kicked off with a flag-raising ceremony at City Hall. However, this civic event was marred by violence on Saturday evening. The deputy police chief, an African American who had proudly marched in the morning's Juneteenth parade, made the decision to shut down the downtown festival three hours earlier than scheduled due to threat of violence. According to reports, two people were stabbed and nearly fourteen arrested, most of them teenagers.

Perhaps there is no story more illustrative of the cycle of violence that summer than the events that resulted in the murders of two Black youths. According to news accounts, Michael Regis and his brother had been in an eight-month dispute with Javon Harris. On Thursday, May 31, 2007, two days before our first workshop, Michael was stabbed to death on South Salina Street, a main thoroughfare along the South Side. Three days later, Javon turned himself in to the Syracuse police at a local South Side church. Javon had been a victim of a multiple stabbing in an unrelated case a year prior.

The following Wednesday, Javon was released on a $10,000 bail bond. Three weeks later on Thursday, June 21, 2007, he was shot and killed by Michael's sixteen-year-old cousin. Javon bled to death two blocks from where he confessed to murdering Michael Regis. Makeba, one of the participants, was related to one of the slain young men. Her pain was quite evident during a workshop, just days after his wake. Makeba's visible distress reflected her fresh grief and the lingering pain of those left behind: the mothers, sisters, cousins, girlfriends, and daughters. The two young men, whose lives were cut short by anger and impulse, appeared side-by-side in photos in the local newspaper that chronicled this catastrophic chain of events.

The summer of 2007 was a time of discovery within the multipurpose room of the local public health center and of racial pride in the city's celebration of African liberation. Yet it was also marked by pain and senseless death. It is against this backdrop that the South Side moms in this project began a dialogue about the lives in their neighborhood. Yet, it is important to move beyond that turbulent summer and trace the historical roots of racial and class formation of the South Side. The next chapter will chronicle the persistent cycles of disruption and dislocation of Syracuse's African Americans, which led to the neighborhood's present concentration of poverty and social problems.

3

Disruption and Dislocation
of Black Spaces in Syracuse

We tore down a row of houses in the old 15th Ward and put up Everson
Muscum . . . I think the change was worthwhile.
—Former Syracuse Mayor William F. Walsh,
nearly thirty years after urban renewal

In my capacity as a Greenpeace campaigner, I was invited to become part
of a mobilization to halt the licensing of a new nuclear-materials enrichment facility in northern Louisiana. The citizen's group was called CANT,
Citizens Against Nuclear Trash, and they were based in Homer, Louisiana. Perhaps the most extraordinary element of this campaign was the
diverse racial composition of CANT. Black and white neighbors rallied
together to oppose the facility in an area where the local Ku Klux Klan
still sponsored marches on the town square during the month of February. A consortium of European and American nuclear companies had proposed building a facility that would enrich uranium for use in fuel rods for
nuclear power plants. Plans for the facility included a road that bisected
two historic African American neighborhoods, Forest Grove and Center Springs. These communities were founded by newly freed slaves after
Emancipation. In the plans for the facility construction, there is not one
mention of the neighborhoods' residents. Fueling the residents' ire, the
map for the planned road did not even bother to include the names and
boundaries of Forest Grove and Center Springs (Bullard 1998). To the
planners, these historic communities were deemed invisible. This blatant

disregard to the presence of African American space and to other spaces occupied by people of color gives testament to the treatment of racial and ethnic minorities by those in power. I see a direct correlation between the assumptions of those who design maps or plans of territories and their views of the people of color that occupy parts of those spaces. This is the type of process, I believe, that leads to the formation of racialized space.

Defining Racialized Space and Environmental Racism and Injustice

Ignoring the historic Black communities of Forest Grove and Center Springs in the plans to construct a nuclear plant in northern Louisiana is a prime example of a process that I refer to as *racialized space,* which illustrates the interplay of space, social relations, and power. I define racialized space as the historic practice and spatial designation of a particular area for racial and ethnic minorities as a means of containment and social control. This practice serves to reinforce preconceived notions of Otherness or results in the creation of culturally inferior Other (Ducre 2006, 2007).

The key assumption of the racialized space hypothesis is that, historically, the mobility of people of color has been (at times) individually sanctioned or constrained through institutional discrimination. I am not the first to put forth the idea of racialized space. However, I believe that my approach is the most comprehensive, taking into account both the influence of racist thought and discriminatory action. For Bill Lawson (2001) and Charles Mills (2001), racialized space constitutes the dominant group's affirmation of Otherness. Thus, their articulation of racialized space encompasses the idea of racist thought as praxis. They contend that Blackness has been equated with evil in a dichotomy against white, which is regarded good and pure. For Lawson, the process of racialization is the mechanism by which conceptualizations of racial superiority are organized in social life and experience. Hence, attitudes regarding urban (Black) versus suburban (White) socio-spatial relations also become racialized: "For many persons, their understanding of the patterns of behavior associated with a racial group is connected with space, giving meaning to the differences in lifestyles and standards of living based on a racial criterion" (2001, 48). Mills (2001) goes further by introducing the dichotomy between Black and white within the body politic as one culturally superior and inferior, organic and inorganic, essential and nonessential. He contends that space is constructed by relations of power and that it is constructed discursively. Thus, if the Other is somehow demonized, containment as a strategy becomes critical. The racist attitudes behind the politics of containment are seen as a protection strategy against the scourge of evil. The distance can be physical, such as the separation of affluent suburban residents from inner city ghetto residents, or mental, such as viewing housing project residents as lazy, criminal, menacing, and intellectually inferior.

In regard to the African American experience, Douglas S. Massey and Nancy A. Denton (1993) conclude that these deliberate containment practices have resulted in the hypersegregation of Blacks, which sets their experiences apart from other racial and ethnic minorities. Accordingly, they contend that Blacks are isolated on all of the five dimensions of geographic segregation: uneven, isolated, clustered, concentrated, and centralized. *Unevenness* is characterized by a population distribution of over- and underrepresentation of racial minorities. *Isolation* refers to the low probability of sharing interracial neighborhoods. A *clustered* geographic space is a dense area predominated by one racial minority, while *concentrated* space not only is dense but also small. *Centralized* refers to the creation of geographic space so distinct that it becomes identified as the urban core.

The preceding arguments address the idea of racialized space as they relate to white separatism that leads to, and is informed by, the partitioning of spaces between white residents and the poor and racial minorities. Conversely, other scholars limit their conceptualization of racialized space to the political economy of space from a neo-Marxian perspective. Massey and Denton (1993) articulate how private actions and institutional policies work together to create urban ghettoes. Even the early work of the Chicago School of Sociology presented the idea of racialized space in their emphasis on human ecology and the race relations cycle and how this process is linked spatially within zones of the center city (Park et al. 1967).

One key practice inherent in the racialized space hypothesis is the persistence of racial residential segregation. Massey and Denton note that racial residential segregation was not a historical accident. Rather, segregation was the result of "actions and practices that had the passive acceptance, if not the active support, of most whites in the United States" (1993, 15). The first collective actions against Black encroachment into white space resulted in violent resistance. Major cities with burgeoning new populations of Southern Black migrants saw race riots at the turn of the twentieth century. The riots were reactions to the steady stream of Black migrants into New York in 1900, East St. Louis in 1917, and Chicago in 1919. Later, more organized efforts came in the form of neighborhood improvement organizations and homeowner associations. Homeowners worked formally to bar the sale and rental of homes to Blacks and other ethnic minorities, using restrictive covenants, restrictive deeds, incorporation, and even zoning (M. Davis 1992; Massey and Denton 1993; Wright 1981). Restrictive covenants were enforceable agreements made between property owners that prohibited the sale or rental of their property to nonwhites for a specified period of time, typically twenty years. These covenants began to appear around the turn of the twentieth century and persisted until the Supreme Court declared them unconstitutional in 1948. Prior to the use of restrictive covenants, individual landowners had created deed restrictions for similar purpose until the Supreme Court struck this practice down in 1917. However, it was not until the formal creation of restrictive covenants that entire neighborhoods were organized to prevent the entry of nonwhites. Mike Davis (1992) referred to these acts as a form of privatized Jim Crow, which succeeded in erecting exclusive white walls in Los Angeles during the 1930s and 1940s.

After the legal defeat of restrictive covenants, some affluent suburban communities favored a new form of white separatism by flexing their political power and lobbying for incorporation and rezoning. By 1930, close to a thousand cities, towns, and villages all over the United States had adopted some form of zoning ordinance, impacting more than 46 million people. Typical ordinances precluded the construction of multiple unit dwellings, restricted lot size, and contained other prohibitive acts that would limit occupation of low-income residents. The private actions of landowners and home associations set the stage for institutional policies that continued the pattern of spatial isolation of minorities. Meanwhile, the suburbanization of white America increased dramatically. Federal programs, such as the Home Owners' Loan Corporation (HOLC) and urban renewal projects emerged out of the racist ideologies of the defunct restrictive covenants.

Charles Mills writes, "Segregation by law is the clearest manifestation of the physical control of the space of an inferior group, a group excluded from full membership in the polity, a group that must be morally, politically, and physically contained" (2001, 85).

To demonstrate the practice of racialized space and the structural reorganization of space by those in power, I will present historic maps and images of Syracuse that illustrate the cycles of disruption and dislocation of African Americans in the city. Why did I choose maps to explore racism and injustice in Syracuse? I relied on the writing of critical cartographer Jeremy W. Crampton (2010) who notes that there is an inherent politic to mapping. Mapping produces specific knowledge and reveals unexamined assumptions held by those in power. Mapping has been used to legitimize and deploy that power. Critical cartographers call attention to the power, knowledge, and assumptions embedded within those maps. They understand that those physical maps have been shaped by historical, political, and economic forces. As an example of critical cartography, Crampton highlights the spatial project of Christopher Columbus, whose myth of American discovery persists:

> By reinscribing new identities on these places, then, and specifically Western Christian names, Columbus effectively created a new space that was compliant with Western beliefs, and which permitted it to be governed and controlled . . . a classic episode in the history of cartography and colonialism. (Crampton 2010, 47–48)

Crampton points out the colonial project to discover, claim, and name spaces circumscribed as "new," despite the presence of indigenous people and culture. Although Columbus and his reclamation of the Americas is one of the most blatant examples of the power to reorganize space, the trend to rediscover, reclaim, and rename persists. Under the guise of "planning," municipal growth machines continue to reorganize spaces in the name of prosperity, at the sacrifice of marginalized Others.

Cycles of Disruption and Dislocation: Racialized Space in Syracuse

Brett Williams (2001) presents a chronology of the growth machine and the emergence of environmental racism in her case study of the predominantly Black Anacostia River neighborhood of Southeast Washington, DC. Williams describes the impacts of residential segregation, suburbanization, pollution from the Navy Yard, and commercial industry along the Anacostia River upon its residents. She starts with the history of Anacostia dating back eleven thousand years ago. The primary actor in facilitating the emergence of environmental racism in Anacostia was the federal government's land speculation and expansion. The District was subject to the whims of federal powers for most of its political history. With each new phase in national identification, the city would undergo massive changes. These changes were ultimately destructive to the Black population. For example, the nation's military mobilization during World Wars I and II caused the expansion of naval operations along the Anacostia River. Subsequently, the navy released massive amounts of chemical contaminants into its waterways. In the decades of urban renewal, many of the District's Blacks were relocated. Williams offers a bit of hope and cites an example of Black agency in the establishment of the Seafarers' Yacht Club. This was the first African American boat club in the nation, which Mary McLeod Bethune helped to launch in her capacity as President Franklin D. Roosevelt's aide.

In the case of Syracuse, there is a common misperception that massive displacement of the city's African Americans occurred in the 1960s under urban renewal programs. However, my research indicates that disruption and dislocation of African American neighborhoods began as early as 1935, with the slum clearance of the Washington-Water Strip neighborhood, reached its peak during the era of urban renewal, and continued as recently as 2005 with the construction of a wastewater treatment plant in the South Side. Thus, this cycle of disruption and dislocation of Black Syracuse has been occurring for nearly seventy years. This chapter attempts to chronicle all three periods of disruption. The next chapter will show evidence from my project's community mapping exercise that, despite the persistence of Black dislocation, place-making is alive and well in the predominantly African American community of the South Side.

The Roots of the Black Community in Syracuse

The earliest accounts of African Americans in Syracuse were of two unknown runaway slaves in 1774 (B. Davis 1980). Their sighting took place not only before the American Revolution but also prior to the city's founding by Ephraim Webster and Asa Danforth around 1784. The two former slaves were engaged in salt mining, which would later become the city's bedrock industry. In 1825, Syracuse became an incorporated village. Its first known Black settler is often identified as "Uncle Ike" Wales. Wales was born a slave in Maryland and arrived in Syracuse as the property of John Fleming in 1810. He eventually bought his freedom from his work on the construction of the Erie Canal for $80 (Stamps and Stamps 2008). On July 4, 1827, the State of New York proclaimed the abolition of slavery. The Black population was still quite small, despite the fact that Syracuse and the surrounding areas were home to the nation's staunchest abolitionists. By the 1860s, Blacks made up only 1 percent of the city's residents. They were concentrated in an area south of the newly built Erie Canal in the sixth, seventh, and eighth wards. The population remained stable, between three hundred and four hundred residents. By the turn of the twentieth century, the Black population reached more than one thousand residents, but there was an overall decline in its proportion to all of Syracuse's residents as whites immigrated to the bustling city at greater numbers (B. Davis 1980; Stamps and Stamps 2008). Although the population climbed steadily, the overall proportion of the African American population to the rest of the city did not increase.

The construction and subsequent success of the Erie Canal system brought economic prosperity to newly arrived white Syracusans, while its Black laborers were primarily relegated to domestic and service jobs. Not only was there strict segregation among occupations but there was also strict racial residential segregation. Black Syracusans were plagued with the same challenges to residential integration as Blacks in other cities across the nation, most notably restrictive covenants. The Great Northern Migration that began in the 1930s saw Blacks migrate from the South to Northern industrial cities at unprecedented rates. This migration didn't affect Syracuse until the 1940s: there was a 120 percent increase in the Black population between 1940 and 1950. Between 1950 and 1960, there was a 144 percent increase (Stamps and Stamps 2008). Blacks lived in two primary areas: Washington-Water Strip and the city's fifteenth ward, a diverse neighborhood of Black and Jewish residents that had some degree of stability.

Although some scholars refer to the 1960s and the period of urban renewal as the source of Black community dislocation, the first forced removal of African Americans occurred some thirty years before urban renewal, in the small section called Washington-Water Strip in 1935. A 1937 survey of the Black community provided a detailed illustration of the communities that made up Black Syracuse (see Figure 3.1).

Darby (1937) describes this small area of about nine blocks in Syracuse's ninth ward, comprised of recent southern Black migrants. Around the same period of the neighborhood survey, city leaders declared the area a slum and issued orders to demolish many of the houses along Washington-Water Strip. Residents were forced to move into the nearby fifteenth ward, increasing its overall population density and further stressing its already deteriorating housing stock.

While one of the only two Black neighborhoods in Syracuse was being demolished, the federal government was conducting comprehensive

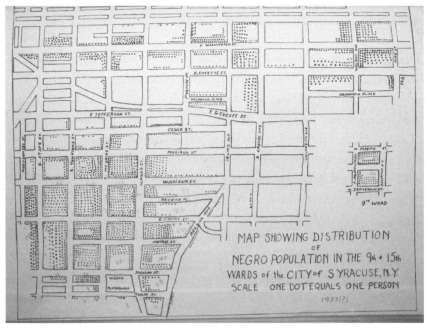

3.1. Map showing distribution of Negro population in the ninth and fifteenth wards of Syracuse. Courtesy of Golden Darby (1937).

surveys of housing and neighborhoods to assess mortgage risk. This effort was led by the Home Owners' Loan Corporation (HOLC), who surveyed more than two hundred American cities between 1935 and 1945. HOLC was a New Deal program whose purpose was to make home financing easier through low-interest loans and uniform mortgage payments. The home finance system for urban residents was founded on a ratings system based on potential risks of mortgage default. Areas determined to have the higher mortgage risks became synonymous with areas with higher populations of racial and ethnic minorities. This ratings system influenced subsequent housing initiatives under the Federal Housing Administration and the Veteran's Administration. The practice evolved into what is referred to as redlining. According to Gwendolyn Wright, "explicit endorsement of segregation—by class and race—was not only an outcome of federal housing policies; it was a stated principle in every government housing program" (1981, 219). HOLC sent agents to cities to survey neighborhoods to evaluate and grade the areas either A, B, C, or D. Neighborhoods or zones illustrated on a HOLC map are identified by one of the four grades and shaded a corresponding color. Category A is the highest and most desirable grade, and neighborhoods with this rating are shaded green. The next level is grade B, whose areas are shaded blue. Category C areas are shaded in yellow. The last and least desirable neighborhoods are graded D and shaded red. The resulting HOLC surveys, called "security area descriptions," are rich with detail on the agent's general impressions of the neighborhood, what he perceived as the area's detrimental influences, the primary race, ethnicity, and occupations of its residents, along with the quality of the housing stock and numerous other variables. Some urban researchers claim that this HOLC mapping system and its color scheme is the origin for redlining. Thus, it can be argued that HOLC and the federal government are the source for what many have assumed were the bank and lending industry's discriminatory practices. Many scholars are critical of the racial legacy of the HOLC maps (Aalbers 2006; Hillier 2003, 2005; Jackson 1987; Sugrue 1996). The HOLC map for Syracuse is featured in Figure 3.2.

The greater Syracuse area—which includes rural and suburban towns of Dewitt, Camillus, Nedrow, Solvay, and Geddes—is divided into

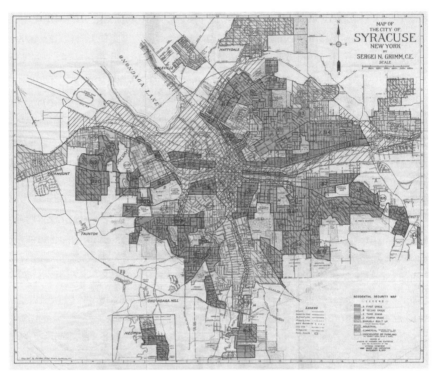

3.2. Records of the Federal Home Loan Bank Board, Home Owners' Loan Corporation, 1933–51, map for Syracuse, 1937. Courtesy of National Archives, College Park, Maryland.

forty-nine distinguishable zones. Five were designated grade A, twenty were rated grade B, and eighteen were given grade C. Six areas were redlined, given the lowest rating of grade D. This survey, dated December 6, 1937, documents the presence of Black Syracusans in only two zones: one section marked as the Negro section and the Townsend Street Section. Both of these zones are given a D rating. The Townsend Street section, labeled D-5 in Figure 3.2, lies adjacent to the Syracuse University campus and next to downtown. A security area description form that accompanies the grade map notes an "influx of Negros" [sic] as one of the zone's detrimental features. The surveyor estimated that 30 percent of the area's population was Negro, with the trend toward increasing numbers of African Americans, which the form categorized as an "infiltration." The area description shared the sentiments of other planning documents from the period, characterizing poor areas of the city as dense and plagued by deteriorating housing stock. Approximately 30 percent of housing stock was multiple-occupancy or tenements, with an additional 30 percent listed as double-occupancy residences.

The most damning statement about the Townsend Street zone can be found in the final section of the form. The surveyor sums up the area as follows: "A very old and quite congested section of the city containing everything from singles to tenements. All are in rather poor condition and display no pride of ownership. *Inhabitants, largely Semitic and Negro, are of an undesirable, laboring type*" (Home Owners' Loan Corporation 1937, italics added). This presupposed lack of pride is also echoed in the other zone where 95 percent of its residents are Black. This section of the city is located in zone D-3. The surveyor remarked that this area is "probably the oldest residential section of the city" and that "there is an air of considerable congestion and complete lack of pride in ownership." These passages are not underscored for its white supremacist language. Obviously, this was written in an era before political correctness. This passage is critical when juxtaposed with what is considered the favorable feature of this same neighborhood: its optimal proximity to the central business district of Syracuse. These two ideas, the supposed inferiority of area's residents and the fact that they live on what planners considered prime property, set the stage for their subsequent removal. The grade ratings in Figure 3.2 combined with the details from the area security description for the Townsend Street and Negro section neighborhoods lend themselves to critical examination of the intentions of the city's growth machine. Did the surveyor's disparaging comments about the inferiority of these neighborhoods and its residents provide a justification for redevelopment of the area? Did the perceived "lack of pride" by the section's residents absolve the city's commitment to provide adequate new housing for the displaced residents in these areas? By the time of the HOLC survey there were slightly fewer than two thousand Blacks in the city. The Washington-Water Strip had been demolished, with most former residents moving to the fifteenth ward. Shortly after the slum clearance of the Washington-Water Strip, the Housing Authority began to plan demolitions within the fifteenth ward. The city's bulldozers seemed to follow Black Syracusans. Research at the Onondaga Historical Association has uncovered correspondence between city leaders to "celebrate" the demolition in 1938:

> Dear Mr. Chase . . . The Syracuse Housing Authority is planning to demolish the first house on its site on Friday, May 20th at 10 A.M. We cordially invite you to be present at the ceremony which will take place at 911 South Townsend Street, and to attend a luncheon to be held in the Tudor Room of the Onondaga Hotel at 12:15 following the ceremony. (Greene 1938, 1)

3.3. *Syracuse Journal* photos captioned, "They Were on Hand for Project's Start," May 20, 1938. Used with permission of *Syracuse Post-Standard*.

Recall that less than a year earlier, Townsend Street received a D rating from the HOLC map survey. Two days after this correspondence, the *Syracuse Journal* published two photos captured at the demolition site, as seen in Figure 3.3. The top photo shows the author of the letter above, Orville H. Greene, acting chairman of the Syracuse Housing Authority, with Mayor Rolland B. Marvin and other city leaders smiling jubilantly at the site on Townsend. Directly below this photo is another whose caption reads, "residents of area watch project begin with wrecking." This image is almost opposite in tone from the photo of the city leaders. The men, including a lone African American, are caught in profile, staring at the demolition in action. Their faces are intent; their mood is somber (*Syracuse Journal* 1938).

That portion of Townsend Street was cleared for the construction of the Pioneer Homes Public Housing complex. Known today by the mothers in the Photovoice project as "The Bricks," Pioneer Homes remains the city's largest block of low-income housing. It opened its doors, primarily to white families, in 1939 and today is the only lasting legacy of the old fifteenth ward (Sieh 2003).

"Urban Renewal Is Negro Removal"

Mindy Fullilove (2004) estimates that approximately 1,600 African American communities were bulldozed under the auspices of urban renewal programs. She describes the pain of destruction on both Black individuals and the Black community in the United States overall as *root shock*: a prolonged stress reaction to the disruption of one's environment or emotional ecosystem. Syracuse's urban renewal program displaced nearly 1,300 people, predominantly Black residences and small businesses, in the fifteenth ward to make way for civic projects. Beginning in the 1950s, the Near East Urban Renewal Project was spearheaded by Syracuse Mayor William F. Walsh. Mayor Walsh acquired federal funds for demolition and slum clearance and paved the way for millions of dollars of downtown development that can still be seen today: the Everson Museum of Art, Upstate Medical Center, the Presidential Plaza project for middle-income housing, a city police station, and two parking lots. Sandra Lane (2008) describes the urban renewal program in Syracuse as tantamount to "ethnic cleansing." Seymour Sacks and Ralph Andrews (1974) report that from 1960 to 1971, 3,689 families and individuals were forced from their homes through various governmental initiatives. Urban renewal and highway construction were responsible for most of the dislocation, affecting 1,660 and 774 residents, respectively. Nearly four hundred families were displaced preceding construction for the Upstate Medical Center and the Department of Mental Hygiene. The third highest form of family disruption was homes destroyed by code enforcement. Figure 3.4 shows a 1954 rendering by the Syracuse Redevelopment Area of presumed fire and health code violations. Like the policies governing the first slum clearance of the Washington-Water Strip, Syracuse civic leaders agreed that the physical deterioration of buildings in the predominately Black neighborhood served as an opportunity for demolition and redevelopment.

There are two prominent spaces in Figure 3.4. Most obvious is the Pioneer Homes Project, bordered by Townsend, Adams, Renwick, and East

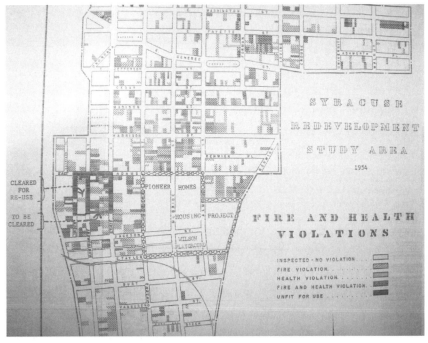

3.4. Syracuse Redevelopment Study Area map, Fire and Health Violations, 1954. Used with permission of Onondaga Historical Association.

Taylor Streets. One block to the east of Pioneer Homes is an area in bold-face: the blocks between Adams and one block north of Jackson. This area has been designated "cleared for re-use." The map is drawn based on the assumption that this area presents one of the densest spaces for fire and health violations. A critical, or perhaps cynical, eye would question the redevelopment agency's evidence of the substandard quality of buildings within this area. The corresponding key suggests that buildings in the highlighted area either have no violation, fire violation, health violation, or fire and health violation. There is considerable agreement, but no indisputable facts available, that the city government determined areas to be slums to drive down the costs of acquiring properties to spur redevelopment. The area slated for clearance in this map does not appear to have more fire and health violations than any other. A wider view of this area is provided in Figure 3.5, a 1955 rendering of the Urban Renewal Plan by the City Planning Commission.

This map still captures the area around Pioneer Homes and includes Syracuse University. The same area adjacent to the public housing complex

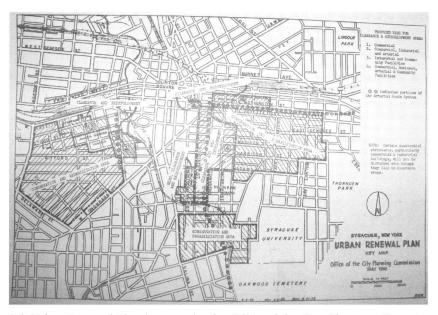

3.5. Urban Renewal Plan key map by the Office of the City Planning Commission, Syracuse, New York, May 1955. Used with permission of Onondaga Historical Association.

is designated for clearance. Examine State Street in Figures 3.4 and Figure 3.5. In Figure 3.4, the clearance area is bounded by State Street to the east. Following northward toward Syracuse's downtown, the area adjacent to State Street has been declared reserved for "conservation and rehabilitation." Likewise, the area adjacent to Syracuse University (and south of the clearance area) has also been designated for "conservation and rehabilitation." These designations seem to mark the conditions of urban renewal: clearance and redevelopment or conservation and rehabilitation. Figure 3.6 clarifies the plans under urban renewal.

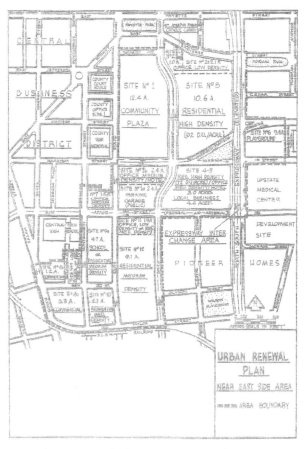

3.6. Urban Renewal Plan, Near East Side Area, Syracuse, NY, undated. Used with permission of Onondaga Historical Association.

In Figure 3.6, the "conservation and rehabilitation" area to the north of Pioneer Homes becomes the site plans for Upstate Medical Center, parking garage, offices, hotels, and some high-density residential buildings. This "rehabilitation" plan effectively extends the expanse of the central business district on the west of State Street. The lot next to Pioneer Homes that was marked for clearance in the fire and health violation map (Figure 3.4) and designated for clearance and redevelopment in Figure 3.5 is slated for medium-density residential facilities, a site for commercial operations, and a proposed school. However, the most visible development was the plan identified on this map as the North-South Expressway. This elevated portion of Interstate 81 bulldozed its way through the heart of the once-bustling community of the fifteenth ward, home to 90 percent of the city's African American population. The map depicts how the expressway effectively severs the Pioneer Homes project in half on what was originally Almond Street.

Figure 3.7 shows the demolition of a section of Pioneer Homes in 1965 to make way for Interstate 81.

A year prior to this demolition, there was a public protest near Pioneer Homes to voice disapproval of plans to temporarily locate a Greyhound Bus Terminal across the street from the housing project. Concerned

HIGHWAY BOWLS OVER HOMES. The section of Pioneer Homes along the west side of Almond street is being demolished to make way for Interstate Route 81. Contractors are clearing the location of the express highway from Raynor avenue to E. Genesee street preparatory to construction work. Pioneer Homes was the first public housing project in Syracuse about 25 years ago.

3.7. *Syracuse Herald Journal* photo of Pioneer Homes demolition, 1965. Used with permission of *Syracuse Post-Standard*.

neighbors brought a petition to Mayor Walsh. By the time the interstate elevation was built, most of the white families had moved from Pioneer Homes. The demographics of the public housing project shifted from predominantly white to predominantly Black residents (Sieh 2004). There is no doubt that this shift in the predominant race of the residents came in response to the clearance and reclamation of other areas in the city where Blacks could live. Although the city created a relocation office for those dislocated by the massive demolition, they did not address the practice of racial residential discrimination. Most white homeowners would not rent or sell their homes to African Americans. Thus, many of those fifteenth-ward residents moved farther south and settled into the South Side where they remain today (Monk 1989).

The quote that opens this chapter is from Mayor Walsh, who seemed unapologetic about the wholesale disruption of Black life in Syracuse, even after thirty years. His refrain is typical of those who helped run the growth machine:

> We tore down a row of houses in the old 15th Ward and put up Everson Museum . . . I think the change was worthwhile. If you want to build up downtown, you've got to provide something down there. If you want to build up the neighborhood, you have to have jobs so people can move into the neighborhood. You build your economy, and people will come. (Sieh 2003, B1)

Stamps and Stamps (2008) note that construction of Interstate 81 spurred land clearance and led to the disruption and dislocation of the Black community residents in both the fifteenth and sixteenth wards. When the demolition dust cleared, 103 acres had been lost. City leaders proclaimed that the path of the interstate had been chosen as the least disruptive in land choices. However, 80 percent of the city's Black residents would be affected by this massive urban land clearance. Just as with Forest Grove and Center Springs in the plans for the Louisiana nuclear facility, the spaces occupied by most of Syracuse's Black citizens were ignored and rendered invisible under the gaze of city planners. Figure 3.8 presents the stark reality of the disruption and dislocation of families resulting from the city's urban renewal programs.

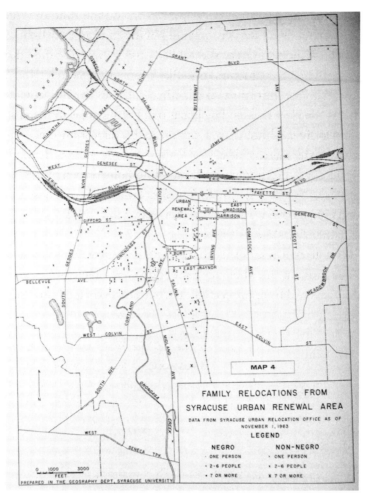

3.8. Family relocations from Syracuse Urban Renewal Area, 1963. Used with permission of Syracuse University, Department of Geography.

The map compares the spatial variation in relocation distance between Black individuals and families versus non-Black individuals and families across the city of Syracuse. The map comes from a 1964 report compiled by University College at Syracuse University. It was produced following civil rights protests in the fall of 1963. Protesters charged that there was rampant housing discrimination after the relocations from urban renewal projects. The report's lead author was Alan K. Campbell, who would later serve as dean of the Maxwell School of Citizenship and Public Affairs at Syracuse University, chair of the U.S. Civil Service Commission, and director of the U.S. Office of Personnel Management under the Carter administration in the 1970s. The other authors were professors from departments across campus, including the law school, economics, geography, and sociology. The report acknowledges African Americans' concerns about housing relocation problems as a result of urban renewal, but the authors chide protesters for oversimplifying the problem plaguing the city's Blacks. They note that housing issues are a result of larger economic conditions of Blacks in the city, most notably low wages, an inadequate education system, and lack of job opportunities. Figure 3.8 relies on data from the Syracuse Urban Relocation office. Blacks tended to relocate near the original urban renewal area, but whites were able to relocate farther away. Moreover, the report points out that, although all those displaced reported rent increases after their relocation, Black families generally paid a higher proportion of their income toward rent when relocating than did non-Black families (Andrews and Campbell 1964). The average rent for Black families prior to relocation was $55.79 per month. After relocation, the monthly rent increased to $66.07. Non-Black families paid an average monthly rent of $46.27 before relocation and $55.90 after relocation. By 1963, 748 families had been displaced by urban renewal and highway construction; 575 (63.7 percent) were African American.

Discriminatory housing practices exacerbated the tolls of disruption and dislocation for many displaced Black families. It was extremely difficult to find reasonably priced, quality housing. Stamps and Stamps (2008) point out that the difficulties that Blacks faced in relocating stemmed mainly from the shortage of units within the city's public housing along with discrimination in private housing. The result was that Black Syracusans were segregated into the city's least desirable housing. Protests led to the establishment of a relocation office for displaced families. However, there was an imbalance between the number of Blacks needing relocation and the availability of quality housing. Perhaps the most problematic aspect of urban renewal is that the poorest Black families found themselves together in one area, leading to the spatial concentration of the poor in the South Side neighborhood.

Stamps and Stamps (2008) also note that the physical and environmental decline of the South Side in the 1960s was prompted by the construction of Interstate 81, which carved its way right through the neighborhood. Once this section of the South Side was disrupted by highway construction, it spurred the flight of the area's remaining white lower middle class and working class. The white residents who remained were those who could not afford to move. Still facing challenges in finding affordable quality housing in the rest of the city, lower- and working-class Blacks replaced the former white residents in the South Side. Wealthier white residents whose homes were closer to the central business district near downtown sold their houses to white-collar businesses or these homes were ultimately abandoned. The urban renewal spurred a racial shift and economic decline of the South Side that is still evident today.

Recent Disruption and Dislocation:
The Midland Sewage Treatment Plant

In 1988, the Atlantic States Legal Foundation, Inc., a nonprofit organization in Syracuse, sued Onondaga County for violation of the 1972 Clean Water Act. Atlantic States contended that the county sewage systems discharged an inordinate amount of wastewater into Onondaga Lake and its tributaries. Onondaga Lake has gained national distinction of being one of the most polluted lakes in the country. The federal Environmental Protection Agency had declared it a Superfund site. A year after the suit, the U.S. District Court issued a consent order instituting a plan that would require the county to develop a new wastewater treatment and sewage system policy on combined sewer overflows (CSO) that would meet the requirements under the Clean Water Act, called the Municipal Compliance Plan. It took ten years and multiple versions of engineering plans for the county to agree to an Amended Consent Judgment and CSO Long-Term Control Plan. The final plan, signed in 1998, called for a new, large regional sewage treatment plant and twelve-foot-diameter sewage pipeline system along Midland Avenue on the South Side. While other neighborhoods were slated to host small, noninvasive supplemental sites for the county wastewater and sewage treatment plan, the plans for the South Side were the largest and the most environmentally disruptive. By the late 1990s, the neighborhood was also home to other municipal projects: a steam plant constructed and operated by Syracuse University, a city bus garage, an industrial laundry facility, and other light industrial enterprises.

Onondaga County used eminent domain to obtain the land to build the Midland Avenue sewage plant. Adjacent to the plant site was a small public housing complex. Its residents were given ninety days notice of eviction (Clark 2005). At the time of the Photovoice project, all of the families had been evicted, and the streets near the Midland Avenue entrance were closed due to construction. A fence was erected around the abandoned housing complex. In its original environmental assessment report submitted to the Environmental Protection Agency, Onondaga County estimated that only seven families would be displaced by the project. Those seven represented the families residing in the nine-unit residential complex on Oxford Street. By 2006, the number of families evicted as a result of the Midland sewage plant construction totaled forty-five. "They just think of us as waste," says a child quoted in a report compiled by a local citizens group opposed to the Midland sewage treatment plant (Partnership for Onondaga Creek 2006).

South Side resident Henry Clemmons poignantly expresses the cost of this cycle of disruption and dislocation in the Partnership for Onondaga Creek report: his recent eviction from his Oxford Street home represented his third forced removal. First, he had to move during the urban renewal of the 1960s and then again during the construction of the city bus garage. Finally, he was forced to relocate due to the Midland waste treatment facility.

This chronology of maps provides evidence of the link between racialized space and, in the final case of the Midland sewage plant, environmental racism and injustice. So how does racialized space relate to the emergence of environmental injustice? The idea is that communities of color and poor neighborhoods are spatially designated as inferior. Through both de jure and de facto acts of segregation, vulnerable pockets are formed to house the undesired population. In most cases, the undesirables are the poor and people of color. The result is that the spaces and inhabitants are viewed by outsiders in either of two extremes: invisible or hypervisible. Recall the case of Forest Grove and Center Springs, the two historic freedmen communities in northern Louisiana that were not even recognized on the planning maps of the proposed nuclear plant. As with these two ignored communities, racialized space may be perceived as invisible, and policy makers fail to take into account the needs of its inhabitants. While policy makers respond to appeals from corporate and other affluent interests, the voices of the occupants within racialized space go unheard.

At the other extreme, the density of racial and ethnic minorities and those with low socioeconomic status serve to make their communities highly visible to outsiders, thereby reinforcing stereotypes. This results in an ideological binary between Black (and brown) and white space. Those that occupy space outside of the racialized space tend to have monolithic images of those that live within the space. All of these perceptions encourage the development of environmental racism and injustice.

The racialized space framework does not highlight one actor or one process. Rather, it acknowledges the fact that there are multiple actors and simultaneous actions that give rise to environmental inequality. It rises above micro-theoretical approaches that emphasize various state and corporate actors. Instead, it is a macro-perspective that not only encompasses spatial relations but also social and temporal dynamics that allow environmental racism and injustice to emerge. Such a framework speaks to processes, rather than to outcomes. It offers a novel approach: space is an explanatory variable when combined with race and socioeconomic status in the siting of environmental hazards. The underlying assumption is that spaces where people of color and the poor reside are not randomly assigned. Instead, they have been designated through a history of white separatism. In addition, these racialized spaces have been vigorously maintained, constraining the physical mobility of marginalized Others.

There are three major assumptions made in articulating racialized space. First, space is power and it is rooted in conflict (Fainstein 1997). The process of dividing people into distinct zones by race and class constitutes an exercise in power. Moreover, resistance on the part of marginalized

Others can be seen as a contestation of power to resist the construction of racialized space.

The second assumption is that space has a dialectical relationship with social relations. In other words, it informs and is reinforced by the social order. David Harvey (1996) notes that, on the one hand, once a spatial arrangement has been established, it tends to institutionalize all other aspects of social behavior. On the other hand, the social order dictates spatial arrangements.

Finally, contemporary forms of racialized space need not be intentional, given their historical construction. Decisions made today about spaces that were created as a part of past segregationist strategies are in effect racialized. These three assumptions underlying the theory on racialized space allude to the dynamics between power, space, and race relations, past and present.

An excellent example is Laura Pulido's essay, "Rethinking Environmental Racism," in which she links elements of historical geography with white privilege and its influence on environmental racism in Los Angeles. She concludes, "This process highlights not only the spatiality of racism, but also the fact that space is a resource in the production of white privilege . . . although whites must go to ever greater lengths to achieve them, relatively homogeneous white spaces are necessary for the full exploitation of whiteness" (Pulido 2000, 30).

While it took them over a decade to achieve justice, recognition and equality, the Citizens Against Nuclear Trash (CANT) received good news in May 1997. The federal Nuclear Regulatory Commission's Atomic Safety and Licensing Board denied the license of the proposed uranium enrichment facility in Homer, Louisiana, based on the environmental injustice claims brought by CANT. In this case, residents were able to successfully lobby for recognition; they were no longer "invisible." It's important to note that the Black community of Syracuse, in the midst of these cycles of forced removal, engaged in collective resistance to the city's projects, especially with the help of groups like CORE (Congress of Racial Equality) in the 1960s and with the Partnership for Onondaga Creek in the 2000s in opposing the sewage plant. However, collective resistance was difficult when fighting against both political and economic forces in the city of Syracuse and Onondaga County. Perhaps the most compelling and persistent form of resistance is the ability of Black Syracusans to resettle, nurture, and make homes for their families after each cycle of disruption. Despite seventy years of demolition and relocation, this community flourishes. The next chapter highlights how the mothers participating in this project see their community after so many changes.

Exploring Black Mothers' Spatiality through Community Mapping

A 1998 *National Geographic* study revealed that people in the United States have a poor grasp of global geography, particularly young Americans (RoperASW 2002). I suspect that most have extensive mental maps of their local communities. My own community map is quite convoluted, because I moved a lot as a child. My mother and I never lived anywhere longer than two years. As an adult, my map became even more complex; instead of moving within the same metropolitan area of Washington, DC, I moved from state to state, region to region. So, when someone inquires about the nearest retail drug store, I can conjure up images of those stores in Lanham, Maryland; Syracuse, New York; or Atlanta, Georgia.

I assumed that the South Side mothers in this project would have a better grasp of their community geography than I do of mine. In addition to determining how well these mothers could map their community, I felt it was also important to explore the ways they evaluated their landscape in terms of safety and security. The preceding chapter focused on the external forces that shape the South Side neighborhood. This chapter, however, explores the agency of the women who call the South Side their home. To do this, I rely on community mapping. This chapter is an analysis of the community mapping exercise as it makes an empirical case for Black women's spatiality. This methodology characterizes the South Side mothers as agents, rather than victims of those external forces that shape their community. In doing so, we can see how they actively shape their environment and assume control of their surroundings, a concept that I refer to as *place-making*.

Eva-Maria Simms (2008) explored the psychology of place in a predominantly African American neighborhood called the Hill District in Pittsburgh, Pennsylvania. Her goal was to understand the social and cultural impacts of dislocation and displacement caused by racial residential segregation and urban renewal programs. A group of twelve Hill residents, ranging from age twenty-four to eighty-four, were asked to draw maps and provide narratives about their neighborhood when they were ten years old. The result is a rich, multigenerational portrait of a single area. Simms was able to analyze how political and economic forces changed the neighborhood and shaped the lives of young children. She divided her analysis by generations. The first generation included those who were ten between 1930 and 1960. This generation experienced strict racial residential segregation, but their childhood world was quite stable, with a strong sense of belonging (or what she refers to as situatedness), strong peer relations among school-aged children, friendly and lifelong neighbors, and a committed community of adults who watched over the children. The second generation of participants in Simms's study was ten years old between 1960 and 1980, and the third generation was ten between 1980 and 2004. The second generation was the first to see dramatic changes to the landscape of their community, marked by urban renewal programs that demolished sections of the neighborhood and by race riots after the assassination of Dr. Martin Luther King Jr. The third generation grew up following the social upheaval of the 1960s and witnessed a rise in substance abuse, street crime, and gang influence, matched with decreased adult presence in and around the neighborhood. Simms saw that the second and third generation of ten-year-olds experienced a loss of situatedness and communality among their peers and among watchful neighborhood adults. Public spaces among the second and third generations became ominous spaces, marked by danger and insecurity.

Moreover, Simms notes that mothers were significantly affected by this upheaval, as they were unable to rely on the network of adult support that had characterized life in the neighborhood during the first generation. Simms's work takes an ecological approach to understanding not merely the physical changes in the Hill District but also how those changes are manifested in the social fabric of the community.

Beverly Xaviera Watkins's case study of Central Harlem in the latter part of the twentieth century (2000) offers another example of understanding dislocation and displacement from an ecological perspective. Key factors that led to Central Harlem's disintegration included suburbanization; deindustrialization; epidemic diseases like heroin and crack addiction, tuberculosis, and HIV/AIDS; and discriminatory policies related to employment, housing, and unequal distribution of public services. The impact of these forces led to *anomie,* or rootlessness, characterized by weakened ties between leaders, neighbors, networks, and families, which gave rise to an increase in crime and antisocial behaviors.

Nikki Jones's book, *Between Good and Ghetto: African American Girls and Inner City Violence* (2010), describes the strategies that young African American girls employ to navigate the random physical violence in their communities while meeting the social expectations of femininity. These two aims can be at odds. This bifurcation is manifested in the decision either to be a "good girl," assuming the acceptable qualities of a young woman, or to be a "girl fighter," eschewing traditional roles of femininity but gaining a level of freedom to walk around the neighborhood. Jones recounts two survival strategies enacted by young women in the inner city: *situational avoidance* and *relational isolation.* Situational avoidance refers to the young women's tactic of self-imposed confined spatiality. "Good girls," on the one hand, limit their time outdoors, preferring to stay home and virtually never diverging from set paths to church or school or other places besides home. These girls employ situational avoidance to prevent their exposure to potentially harmful situations. "Girl fighters," on the other hand, have greater freedom of mobility because of their perceived ability to hold their own in physical confrontations. Jones defines the term *relationship isolation* as a strategy to inhibit close social relationships, particularly with other women, in the hopes of avoiding physical confrontations that they may be drawn into by defending close friends.

I vividly recall my own experience in navigating space as a young Black woman. One afternoon when I was in middle school, my Aunt Niecey sent me to the local convenience store. Before I could reach the door, a group of young guys emerged from behind the building. This gang was infamously known around my neighborhood as *cherrybusters,* alluding to their sexual violence. Their leader, whom I will call Mike, was older than most of the others. He was an ex-convict I'd seen from a distance and always avoided. But this afternoon, these guys appeared suddenly with Mike in the lead. I ignored their taunts and catcalls and was trying to enter the store when Mike grabbed me from behind. I struggled fiercely, which only served to amuse him and the others. At that point, he held me physically off the ground, with my backside plastered to his front. I feared that he was going to force me to the rear of the building. Fortunately, the other boys did not help him. Some part of my brain screamed at me, "Don't let him take you behind the store!" Mike's hand was covering my face and in a last-ditch effort to free myself, my teeth clamped down on his hand. He dropped me to the ground. He must have cursed me, but I couldn't hear a thing beyond the harsh beating of my heart. I can't recall what happened in the next few seconds. The gang didn't retaliate; they all seemed to fade back to wherever they'd come from. With shaking knees, I went into the store, only to find that the store clerk had seen it all. His conclusion: "Had a fight with your boyfriend, huh?" *I had a fight with my boyfriend?* I told him emphatically that that was *not* my boyfriend. He smirked. I made my purchase and left. When I met my aunt nearby, I didn't tell her about the incident.

Jones's analysis is quite useful in articulating the choices young women must make in navigating inner-city landscapes. I suspect that while the pitfalls of inner city life for African American adult mothers are quite similar, they cannot employ situational avoidance. As caretakers, they are required to move about their environment, regardless of the potential for violence. Implicit in both strategies women use to avoid potential violence is *spatiality*: having a sense of your neighborhood's geography, along with an understanding of the risks and opportunities associated with particular areas. This spatiality allows the young women in Jones's book and the mothers in my project to maximize success while minimizing risks in a particularly risky landscape. In an attempt to understand the South Side mothers' spatiality and place-making, I used the tool of community mapping.

Inspiration for my project's community mapping exercise comes from Cheryl Teelucksingh (2001). She gauges individual awareness of local environmental risk by giving each of her study's participants a map of the local area and asking them to mark the locations of particular resources and land areas, both desirable and undesirable. My community mapping exercise is quite similar. It occurred during the first workshop on Saturday, June 9, 2007. After our introductions and the participants' consent to proceed, we immediately launched into the community mapping exercise. Only ten participants completed this exercise: Billie, Nikki, Makeba, Faith, Gwen, Nina, Shirley, Katherine, Zora, and Harriet. (Josephine, CJ, Elizabeth, and Barbara did not join the group until the second workshop. They were selected randomly as alternates.) I gave each woman a map of the general boundaries that encompass the South Side neighborhood. In addition to the map, I gave them a red pencil and a green pencil. I asked them to use the green pencil to mark those areas within the neighborhood that they felt were safe and healthy places for them and their children. The red pencil was to mark spaces that they considered unsafe and unhealthy. I provided very little direction beyond those initial instructions, because I was very interested to see what evolved naturally. The following section briefly summarizes each participant's mapping.

Billie defines areas on her map with bold multiple rings around them. At first glance, there were a relatively even number of both red-lined and green-lined areas. Her map (Figure 4.1) also shows a peculiar pattern used by other women in the group; in some instances areas are marked by both red and green pencils, such as the Southwest Community Center. Billie's positive areas are typically parks or green spaces. Her positive areas include Onondaga Creek Park, Kirk Park, Onondaga Park, Jubilee Park, amd Roesler Park, along with Castle and State Park. The exception was the red-circled McKinley Park and Baker Playground. Another notable feature is that Billie's negative areas tend to be clustered city blocks, including streets along Bellevue Avenue and a corridor near South Salina Street.

Nikki either neatly shades areas on her map (Figure 4.2) with the red and green pencils or marks them with red or green dots. Like Billie, Nikki shades entire blocks. There also seem to be varying levels of intensity to her shaded areas. For instance, her most intensely red-colored areas are Oxford Street, the South Salina corridor, and the Midland Avenue corridor along with cross streets of West Kennedy and McLennan Avenue. There are more red- than green-shaded areas. Like others, Nikki highlights the contradiction in the Southwest Community Center, marking it both red and

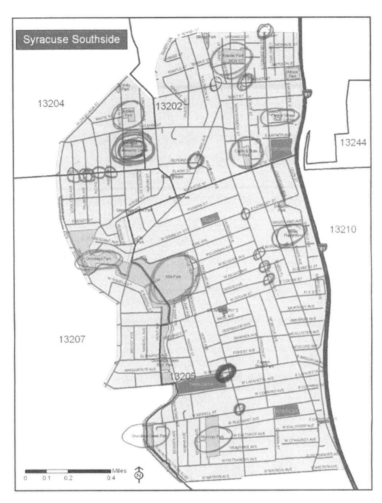

4.1. Billie's map, 2007. Southside Photovoice Project Collection. Used with permission of Jonnell Allen Robinson.

green. Her green areas include some parks, like Roesler Park, Jubilee Park, and Onondaga Park, as well as local schools like Dr. Martin Luther King Jr. Elementary, Danforth Middle School, and McKinley Elementary School. She also marks a spot outside of the South Side boundaries, indicating that my map is not inclusive of the entire community.

Makeba's approach to marking her map (Figure 4.3) is distinguished by oval-shaped circles around the street names. As a result, her map

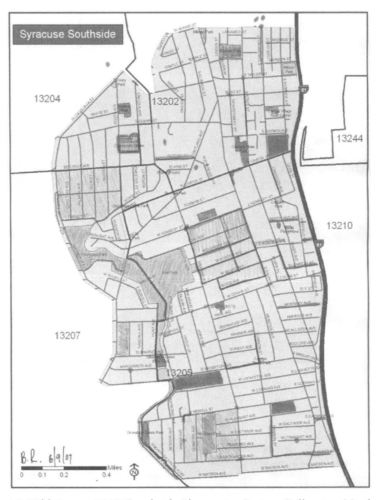

4.2. Nikki's map, 2007. Southside Photovoice Project Collection. Used with permission of Jonnell Allen Robinson.

resembles a series of zones. Two such zones stand out above the others: the red zone around the Bellevue Avenue corridor from Coolidge Avenue to Rich Street, and the eastern end of the South Salina corridor that includes East Colvin Street and Beard Place. Within the red-rimmed South Salina corridor, she marks a green oasis on Borden Avenue. Overall, I see far more red areas on Makeba's map than green ones. Like the other women's maps, Makeba's positive selections include

4.3. Makeba's map, 2007. Southside Photovoice Project Collection. Used with permission of Jonnell Allen Robinson.

the neighborhood parks and institutions such as the McKinley Elementary School. She also presents the contradiction of the Southwest Community Center. On her map, its name is enveloped by slashes of green and red pencil lines. However, Makeba draws both red and green ovals around Billings Park in the northernmost point of the South Side and around West Brighton Avenue, immediately above Danforth Middle School as well.

Faith's markings are faint, no wild slashes or circles. The only heavily shaded red area that jumps from the page is an area bounded by West Beard Avenue, Wood Avenue, Midland Avenue, and South Salina Street. Faith's intentions are quite precise. The eye is drawn to that shaded area right in the middle of the map. But careful observation reveals that there are more positive areas on Faith's map than negative ones. Unlike others, Faith's map doesn't include any positive designations for more formal institutions or green spaces, and she marks the Southwest Community Center as solely green, a positive place. Like Nikki, Faith identifies an area that is outside the boundaries of the map. Faith's other positive places include Jubilee Park and the South Avenue corridor that runs from Jubilee to the Southwest Community Center, Burt and Montgomery Streets, and the block of streets around Dr. King School. Negative locations include West Kennedy Street at Midland Avenue, South Salina, and Colvin, and the area surrounding Cannon Street Park.

Gwen's approach to mapping the South Side neighborhood matches her demeanor during all of the project's workshops. There are no wild slashes or shaded areas; she meticulously presents simple red and green dots to highlight different areas. When denoting an entire corridor as negative, she draws a single line that connects the red dots. Just as she used her words sparingly during the workshops, she also used the colored pencils sparingly. There are very few stray marks or scratches. However, there are more red dots on Gwen's map than on the others'. Like Nikki and Faith, Gwen's positive areas include some outside the boundaries of the map. Other positive areas include South Avenue near Trinity Park, Jubilee Park, Central Village Youth Center, the intersection between Burt and Montgomery Streets, and Dr. King School. She marks the Southwest Community Center in both red and green. Like other women, Gwen identifies the Bellevue Avenue corridor as an unsafe space. However, at the end of Bellevue, near West Onondaga Street, she notes a positive area. What strikes me about Gwen's map are the contradictions: the close proximity of her desirable areas to her undesirable areas. For example, near her green designation of Jubilee Park is the red area of South Avenue and Tallman. She labels Dr. King School as green but the street adjacent to the school is red. There are adjacent red and green dots on Midland Avenue near West Newell. This signals that she can't avoid certain areas in the South Side. Most likely, she has to travel through undesirable areas to get to the better portions of her community. Her undesirable areas are similar to those of other women in the group.

Nina has bold splashes of color on her map (Figure 4.4). She colors everything, making quite a chaotic visual of the South Side. She shades in an entire block to denote its safety or danger. There are no single-colored streets; all the markings are bounded on all four sides. Like others, Nina selects some of the areas' parks as positive spaces. However, she also notes other public spaces for their questionable safety: Southwest Community Center, Kirk Park, McKinley Park, Castle and State Parks, and Baker Playground. It may be useful to note that unlike others' patterns, Nina did not mark any schools or community centers green. Her other positive spaces include the Oakwood Avenue corridor, McKinley Avenue between Salina Street and I-81, and an entire section around Marguerite Avenue between Cortland and Hunt Avenues. Nina denotes only five positive spaces on her map, the smallest number among the participants. Instead, there are large swaths of red, including the Lincoln Avenue corridor, the area near Oxford and Cortland Avenue, the block south of the Southwest Community Center on Bellevue Avenue, the South Salina corridor that encompasses West Borden, the area including Baker Playground, and an area near Danforth School.

Shirley neatly drew circles around places that she designates as posi-tive or negative. Many of her choices resemble those of the other women. Shirley chooses Village Youth Center, Kirk Park, Onondaga Park, McKin-ley Park, and the Danforth School as positive. She shows the same con-tradictory feelings about the Southwest Community Center as others, circling the square on the map with both red and green pencils. Other green-marked areas include Burt and Montgomery, Oakwood Avenue cor-ridor, Bishop Avenue between West Colvin and Elmhurst, and portions of Midland Avenue. In the southeastern section of the map she notes in green the place she lives, which unfortunately is outside the boundaries of the map. Her negative places are also quite similar to the others'. She

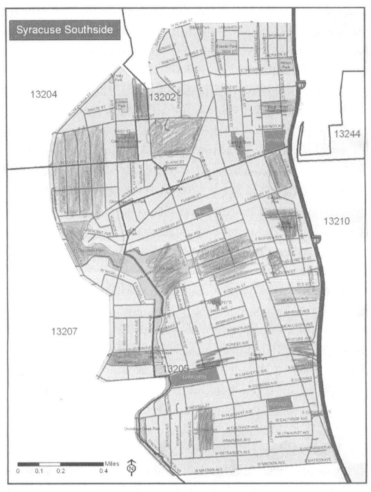

4.4. Nina's map, 2007. Southside Photovoice Project Collection. Used with permission of Jonnell Allen Robinson.

includes an undesirable area outside the map boundaries, along with Tallman and Lincoln, Bellevue Avenue corridor, Onondaga Creek Park, and Oxford Street, to name a few.

At first glance, Katherine has more negative areas than positive ones (Figure 4.5). Furthermore, her choices are consistent with those of the other women. In terms of positive public areas, Katherine chooses the Central Village Youth Center and Kirk Park. She also marks the Burt and

Montgomery Streets location, a popular positive choice. Like the others, she considers the Southwest Community Center both a positive site and a negative one, although the manner in which she indicates this is unique. She colors the area of the center red and then writes in green next to it, "good/bad"—perhaps reflecting the conversation among the group about the relative contradiction of this popular neighborhood center. Another unique labeling feature on Katherine's map is West Bissel Street, where she writes "Home" in green lettering. She also writes and underlines the word, "Home" in an area beyond the map's boundaries. Her negative associations include many of the other participants' choices: the notorious Bellevue Avenue corridor, Onondaga Creek Park, Oxford and Blaine Streets near Cortland Avenue, West Castle near Cortland Avenue, Elk Street, McKinley Avenue near I-81, an area near Cannon Street Park, and McKinley Park.

Like Katherine, Zora uses an interesting strategy in communicating her choices on her South Side map (Figure 4.6). The positive/green areas are denoted with a small "X" in green, while the negative/red areas are colored much more dramatically: the blocks shaded red and their street boundaries underscored with a red outline as well. This results in a map that is vividly accentuated by red/negative areas. In fact, one's eye must search carefully around the map to find the small green Xs, while the bad areas stand out like neon signs. Her large red areas encompass four major "bad zones": (1) the area around McKinley Park, between West Newell and West Ostrander, (2) the Borden, Beard, and Wood Avenue corridor with Midland to the west and South Salina to the east, (3) the Oakwood and Garfield Avenue corridor near I-81 and Baker Playground, which connects to the final zone, right to the north, and (4) the area around Castle and State Park and Dr. King Elementary along South State Street. Like Gwen, Zora marks some green/positive places right in the midst of what she views as dangerous corridors; most notably on Oakwood where she places three green dots along the red-outlined street boundaries of Oakwood. She does the same with a green dot on South Townsend Street within the red zone near the Central Village Youth Center and Castle and State Park. The only negative space that falls outside of these four red zones is the Oxford Street space. Her positive areas include the Southwest

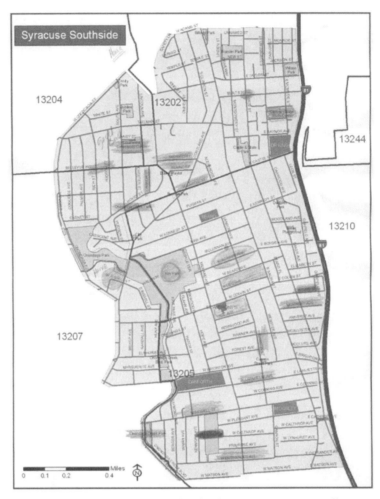

4.5. Katherine's map, 2007. Southside Photovoice Project Collection. Used with permission of Jonnell Allen Robinson.

Community Center (which she marks as solely "green/positive"), Onondaga Park, and Kirk Park. Another positive space can be found on Tallman Street and Oneida Street. In pen, she writes the word "HOME" near Kennedy and Kirk Avenue. However, she does not designate the space either red or green.

Similar to Zora, Harriet's marks consist of green and red Xs on her map (Figure 4.7). Harriet regards institutions as positive spaces. In fact, Harriet's

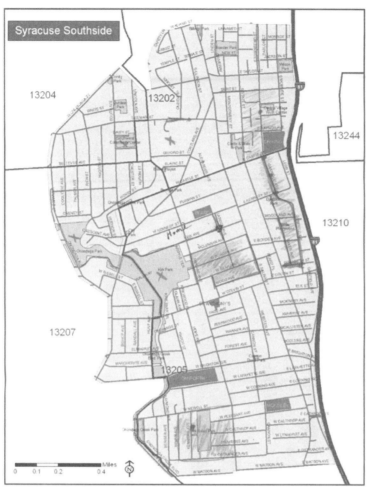

4.6. Zora's map, 2007. Southside Photovoice Project Collection. Used with permission of Jonnell Allen Robinson.

mapping shows a close correlation between positive attributes and green spaces. In addition, Harriet includes Burt and Montgomery Streets as green, and the Taylor and Cortland Street intersection is distinctively circled in both red and green. She marks McKinley Park as a negative space, along with an area near Baker Playground. Other negative places include the Bellevue Avenue corridor, Wood Avenue and West Colvin near Midland, and Oxford Street.

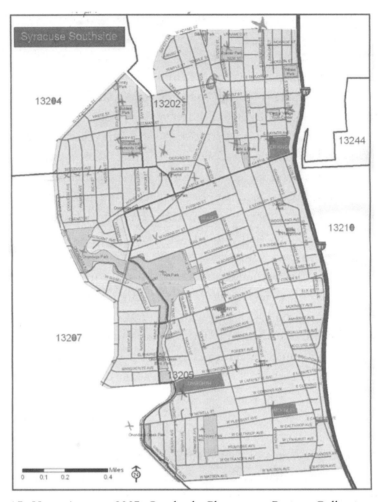

4.7. Harriet's map, 2007. Southside Photovoice Project Collection. Used with permission of Jonnell Allen Robinson.

When all of the women completed their maps individually, the group broke for lunch. After lunch, there was group discussion of their selections and dialogue around their choices. Harriet was the first person to discuss her positive and negative designations. As she started to discuss problems with gang and drug activity in the Bellevue Avenue corridor, the group became more animated and began to talk over one another. Harriet responded to this heightened discussion by shutting down. She announced that I, as moderator, should let someone else talk, because "I can't talk really good." Eventually, with more support on my part, she opened up again. The discussion was so fast-paced that I couldn't keep up. I had the same copy of the map the women used and enlarged it for the group discussion. Eventually Billie volunteered to mark spots that the women discussed on the larger map in the front of the room.

The most frequently cited positive spaces within the South Side were Kirk Park and the Southwest Community Center. Each was cited by eight out of the ten women. Seven women also noted Onondaga Park and the Central Village Youth Center as positive places. And more than half of the women noted the positive aspects of the intersection of Burt and Montgomery Streets, Jubilee Park, and the Oakwood corridor.

Kirk Park. Adjacent to Onondaga Park is the thirty-three-acre area called Kirk Park, shown in Figure 4.8. At the turn of the twentieth century, Kirk Park was considered the city's driving park for horse and bike races (Syracuse Department of Park, Recreation and Youth Programs 2008a). It was also the site of early county fairs. It became a city park in 1910, and today boasts a community center, an outdoor pool, playground, two sports fields, tennis and basketball courts, and a pavilion. Nikki pointed out the amenities at Kirk Park as positive characteristics: "I think that it's good for the kids because it has a lot of stuff they can play around with, [like] basketball, they can interact with each other."

Southwest Community Center. Established more than thirty years ago, the Southwest Community Center sits at 401 South Avenue, in the heart of the South Side community. (The front of the center is marked in Figure 4.8.) Its mission is to empower local residents, and it serves approximately 750 South Side youths annually (Melchiorre et al. 2003). The most common programs at the center include tutoring and gym sports, as well as other cultural and educational activities geared toward youth. Despite being a positive force within the South Side community, the center is a contradiction.

During the same month as our community mapping and Photovoice project, ten gunfire incidents near the Southwest Community Center were reported to the Syracuse police, more than half of all such incidents reported citywide in June 2007 (Dowty 2007). Many of the women marked

4.8. (a) Kirk Park.

4.8. (b) Southwest Community Center.

4.8. (c) Onondaga Park. Photos in 4.8 (a)–(c) taken by author.

it both red and green. Makeba noted, "Inside the Southwest Center is good, but it's a lot of followers here. They're always following the people that's doing the negative activity. They bring the children or the teenagers, they think it's good they doing it so they following them, which is really not good at all." Gwen pointed to the presence of gangs as the sole negative influence around the space inhabited by the center: "They have a lot of gang members hanging outside." Nina said, "The workers that work there—they really try hard for the kids, but most of the kids there; they're following negative footsteps, and they try to bring it in the center. It's not the center. They try really hard to keep it up, they need help. The outside is making it bad. The influences . . . the people inside the youth center are really trying to do their job to make it safe." Shirley jumped into the discussion to defend the Southwest Center: "It's not that the Southwest Center isn't aware of this—because they have police there 24 hours, trying to protect the kids from the neighborhood. But they can't protect them; they can only protect them on the center's grounds, not across the street or down the street."

Shirley's comments strike me in two important ways when examining the neighborhood and its impact on place making. First, I am surprised by the phrase "protecting kids from the neighborhood," which acknowledges the neighborhood as having its own identity and characteristics that give it an objective identity outside of social relations. Here, the neighborhood represents its own menace, which is a very sad indictment. Secondly, Shirley shares a sense of extreme place vulnerability, one in which she claims that police do not have the capacity to keep her or her kids safe from the neighborhood. Who or what can Shirley rely upon to keep her family safe? Katherine echoed a similar fatalist sentiment, "There was a car, I think about a month ago. There was a guy sitting in his car, smack dead in front of the Southwest Center, and he moved right up and shot three kids . . . so like she said [referring to another participant's comments], the Southwest Center, they do positive things, but the minute you step outside, only God knows what can happen."

Castle and State Park provide another case study of the gap between the city leadership and the community residents. Recently this park was renovated to include brand-new, shiny playground equipment, but the women do not feel comfortable with the area surrounding the playground. As Nina pointed out, "You do not send your child there alone, you understand. Somebody just redid it, put new things in it, but to just send your child there is very uncomfortable . . . it's not a good idea." Makeba was not as definitive in her stance on Castle and State Park: "I was there with my brothers and sisters, and it's fine there [but] make sure you watch them." However, she added, "You can always get away from something that happens, but you can't prevent it from not being there." Like Shirley and Katherine's comments about the random violence outside the Southwest Center, Makeba's comments reveal a sense of inevitability that comes with urban violence.

Onondaga Park. This park is divided into Upper Onondaga Park, which lies west of Onondaga Avenue, and the lower portion of the park. One section of this immense green space is shown in Figure 4.8. It covers approximately sixty-seven acres, with a swimming pool, athletic fields, basketball courts, playground, a man-made lake and a gazebo (Syracuse Department of Park, Recreation and Youth Programs 2008c). Nina chose this park as green because of the activities there for her school-aged daughter.

Burt and Montgomery Streets. Shirley was one of the first to express the positive effects of a nondescript but clean and modern beige brick building on the corner of Burt and Montgomery called the *Gateway House* (see Figure 4.9). It is a twenty-four-bed mental health facility that opened in the summer of 2005 amid some community opposition (Mulder 2004). At the time the local newspaper quoted former Syracuse Common Councilor Tom Seals saying that the South Side community was being used as a "dumping ground" (Mulder 2004). No signs distinguish the unassuming building. Shirley acknowledged, "That's where I got clean and sober at and as well that's where my church is." Harriet viewed this area in a positive light because it was where she used to live. Many of the women recalled fondly places where they used to live or where they had a child.

Jubilee Park. The City of Syracuse Department of Parks, Recreation and Youth Programs officially call this the "Spirit of Jubilee" Park. Located along a more commercial area of South Avenue, it is a small park, a little over two acres, featuring a small baseball diamond, a tennis court, and a basketball court (Syracuse Department of Park, Recreation and Youth Programs 2008d). It also has a playground, shown in Figure 4.9. The park hosts part of the annual Juneteenth celebration. Billie said, "I put Jubilee Park . . . that's where they have the little concerts and stuff for the summer. That's where they go after the parade and stuff for Juneteenth. That's where they continue."

Central Village Youth Center. Nikki highlighted this youth center on her map because, "it's good for kids." Nina also chose Central Village because of positive memories of her son's extracurricular activities there. Central Village Youth Center is located amid the Pioneer Homes public housing complex, known in the community as "The Bricks," on the northern edge of the South Side community (see Figure 4.9). Opened in 1989 by the city Housing Authority, the youth center has suffered greatly from the bust and boom cycle of city social service programs. Budget deficits within the Housing Authority forced the center to shut down in June

4.9. (a) Burt and Montgomery Streets.

4.9. (b) Jubilee Park.

4.9. (c) Central Village Youth Center.

4.9. (d) Oakwood Corridor. Photos in 4.9 (a)–(d) taken by author.

2006. Nearly a year later, it reopened under the administration of the Boys and Girls Club (Fish 2006a, 2006b).

Oakwood Corridor. There is more than one institution along the Oakwood Avenue corridor between East Castle and East Kennedy Streets that inspired positive feelings among most of the mothers, including a concentrated presence of several churches. Figure 4.9 presents a street view of the Oakwood corridor. On one end is the Dr. King Elementary School; on the other sits the small Danforth Park. Across the street, near Dr. King, is a one-story complex of low-income public housing. Nikki pointed out the religiosity inherent in the church-lined avenue of Oakwood, but she has a special place for all churches: "I basically want all of the churches I've seen or passed [on the map] . . . I love how there are churches every two blocks." Her comments were seconded by all. "I put Oakwood, like she was saying, it's a church area," recalled Zora. "Like, everybody [has] a church [there]. You can draw a line down Oakwood Avenue."

There was also a high level of agreement about places that the mothers considered negative influences on health and safety. Harriet's comments encapsulated the general sentiment surrounding the selection of the negative areas: drug activity and violence. She noted, "All of my red spots, I haven't experienced, but I know about [them] from watching the news. I'm scared to go into these neighborhoods because of the things that I hear or see in the news. Like we got that whole line on Garfield [Avenue] . . . the Boot Camp [a local gang] is from that area, so I'm scared to go. I don't go on that side of town."

Southwest Community Center appears at the top of the lists for both positive and negative spaces, with 80 percent agreement on it being a negative space. Other locales that elicited 80 percent agreement were the Bellevue Avenue Corridor, Oxford Street, and the South Salina Street corridor. A little more than half of the mothers associated Midland and Brighton Avenues, McKinley Park, and the intersection of Borden and South Salina as negative places.

Bellevue Avenue Corridor. As with the Southwest Community Center, the women agreed that Bellevue Avenue's negative influence is related to gangs. More specifically, one participant points to a local gang called 110. The notorious Bellevue Avenue corridor is one block south of the

Southwest Community Center and stretches along Bellevue Avenue eastward, encompassing the cross streets of Hudson, Rich, Palmer, and Coolidge Avenues. Although the group acknowledged the effectiveness of the concentrated police sweeps of the area, Shirley said that she still avoids the area. She pointed out the unintended consequence of the police sweeps of gangs: new battles over turf by remaining members and rival gangs. She noted, "They [police] got all of the old-heads . . . that means, you know, the over twenty-one or twenty-five in jail. But they got the young ones, seventeen or eighteen out there, taking over. All of them are not in jail. The ones that's in jail, they left ones out here to take over for them."

Oxford Street. The mothers placed the source of tension on Oxford Street (Figure 4.10) squarely on the Oxford Street Inn, a homeless shelter for men run by Catholic Charities of Onondaga County. The founders converted the former Saint Vincent DePaul warehouse into a shelter during Christmas of 1979 (Hawkins 1988). They accept men each night, some of whom are intoxicated and drug-addicted. Each morning, many of the men loiter in the area, which causes a great deal of concern for the mothers. Billie said, "It's a shelter for men, but women and men hang out front, all they do is drink, do drugs, smoke right there out in front of everybody . . . They buy their drugs out there . . . The shelter is closed from 7 in the morning to 7 at night . . . the building is locked." Later, she mentioned an incident where the body of a man was found near the shelter, shot to death. Shirley talked about a store on Oxford Street near the shelter, which has since closed down: "I figured that was a bad place because some mothers are on crack so bad that the store was buying their food stamps, and they was enabling the parents to get their drugs more than what they should have been."

Recall that Shirley is a recovering substance abuser; earlier, she noted the importance of the rehab center on Burt and Montgomery. Imagine the fight that Shirley must overcome, with her resolve to remain sober, having to cope with the daily onslaught of drug abuse within her community. The presence of facilities like the Oxford Street Inn and the Gateway House on Burt and Montgomery offers an interesting dilemma. While these facilities are beneficial in serving the most vulnerable segments of the community, no other neighborhoods are willing to host them. These are what

4.10. Oxford Street (*top*), McKinley Park (*bottom*). Taken by author.

environmental justice advocates call *lulus*: least undesirable land uses. Inevitably, neighborhoods who demonstrate the least amount of resistance become hosts to projects that others are unwilling to accept.

South Salina Corridor. With the exception of highway I-81, which stretches the length of the entire neighborhood to the west, the largest thoroughfare on the South Side is South Salina Street, which serves as the neighborhood's commercial center. For instance, a major furniture retailer has its largest showroom and warehouse on South Salina. A colorful shoe store does business near the furniture showroom. Several mom-and-pop stores dot the street, from a used-furniture store to a boutique featuring wigs and other hair accessories. There is a branch office of a major bank, as well as a busy post office. Syracuse University has recently created the South Side Innovation Center here, a small business incubator for entre-preneurial South Side residents. What is conspicuously absent is a major grocery store, evidence of patterns in health and nutrition inequality noted by public health and environmental justice scholars (Morland et al. 2002; Morland and Wing 2007; Zenk et al. 2005). Despite these commer-cial institutions on South Salina, the women in the project reminded me that parts of the street remain unsafe. Billie said, "I also got Salina because that's where the last two killings [were] . . . the seventeen-year-old that just got shot last week, that's where he got killed at. So all that whole area, I don't mess around." While the actual size of the unsafe corridor on South Salina varied on each woman's map, they consistently agreed that the area on South Salina that encompassed West Borden, West Beard, and Wood Avenues were negative areas.

Midland and Brighton. A number of the women's maps highlighted the intersection of Midland and West Brighton Avenues. It is alarming that Danforth School sits very close to that corner. Zora was quick to note during the exercise that this intersection is similar to an area near Dr. King school: "Yeah, they still doing like they do at Dr. King. I mean, it's close to the school, but over there in the Bricks, they selling drugs left and right."

McKinley Park. McKinley Park (see Figure 4.10) has the distinction of being one of the few green spaces within the South Side that received negative ratings. Despite its promising features—nearly eight acres, swimming pool, baseball field, playground and basketball courts—the women still regarded McKinley as an undesirable space (Syracuse Department of Park, Recreation and Youth Programs 2008b). Along with the identified area of Midland and Brighton and the Bellevue corridor, they associated this park with heavy drug trafficking. Shirley vowed, "I wouldn't let my kids play in it."

In sum, many of the positive spaces the group identified were those associated with personal experiences: places where they lived or worked, where their children attended school or daycare or had extracurricular activities, and where they experienced something positive, such as the birth of a child or recovery. Some positive spaces were chosen because of their aesthetic qualities. They tended to be less crowded areas or green spaces like parks where children could play safely. Related to aesthetics, the women associated the presence of churches with positive feelings. Negative spaces tended to occupy larger swathes of city blocks and were associated with past acts of violence, the potential for future acts of violence, and significant drug trafficking and gang activity.

The mothers have to carefully navigate these areas, always concerned with their safety and, more important, their children's safety. This is difficult, because some of the unsafe spaces are located very close to schools, places of worship, commercial areas, and playgrounds within the neighborhood. At one point in the discussion with the women, I asked, "What are you afraid of, for your children?" I had not heard from Zora up until this point so I directed the question to her. "The worst thing I could imagine happening to my son is him being beaten and me not being able to get ahold of him—something bad happening to him. Or a drive-by shooting, or something like that, you know. And me not knowing something [has] happened to my son." Harriet echoed the same sentiment, reflecting, "'cause a bullet don't have no name," referring to the random violence of a drive-by shooting. She was also concerned about one local park and the fact that young boys hung around it, so she wouldn't let her daughter go there. But Shirley surprised me by taking a conservative stance on the potential for violence:

It's bad to say that you have to keep your kids inside the house because bullets coming through. I guess it's the company you keep. You know if I'm hanging around with Billie, and I know she's doing something [she] ain't got no business [doing], and she hot and they about to get her. And I keep playing around with her, and I get her bullet, then I need to get it cause I know she hot . . . I got nine kids, seven boys and two girls and I tried to teach them, if anything happens to you, it's because somebody in your clique done did something f-ed up and they just be talking about it. I say you need to find out what's going on in your clique before you trying to hang out with your clique. And that's just for me. If I go up to the store, and I get a bullet or something like that, it's somebody they want in my surroundings. And I just pray to God it don't happen and I don't die."

Her statement offers two revelations. One, her viewpoint places accountability for violence on the victim. Thus, if you find yourself in a vulnerable position, it's due to your association with a social network of presumed violence. However, Shirley also allowed for random acts of violence. While she affirmed that she deliberately chose not to associate with persons who are "hot," she acknowledged the unpredictability of her environment (e.g., in going to the store) and admitted that she prayed for divine safety. The second revelation is that Shirley teaches her children a nuanced strategy similar to that presented by Jones in her discussion of situational avoidance and relational isolation. Instead of limiting relationships with others, like the adolescents who were interviewed by Jones in Philadelphia, Shirley advised a strategy of relational isolation when it comes to certain types of individuals. She advocated a strict selection of peers with whom her children should associate themselves. Makeba adopted a stance of situational avoidance: "I don't be outside much, I work a lot." I surmised that Katherine employed a similar stance as Makeba, when she declared, "I'm a home person."

Nina said that her biggest fear was that her child would find drugs or drug paraphernalia. She imagined that this exposure to drugs would lead to willingness to using or selling them. As a parent of a toddler, Gwen also feared that her toddler would find something at the park and put it in her mouth. She referred specifically to a needle used for drugs. (Ironically, Gwen would come across just such a needle one day on the ground while taking photos during the Photovoice exercises of this project.) Zora chimed in with her fears about the exposure to weapons, such as guns. The group's discussion here reveals their awareness of the high prevalence of drug activity, both its use and its distribution in public spaces. This fact weighs heavily on the minds of mothers who have to face this reality while raising their children.

Makeba also shared this concern. She pointed out: "You know how kids like to watch everything. They're looking at everything, so they might think it's a good thing. They might think it's a bad thing." Shifting from the threat of violence and the potential for exposure to drugs and weapons, Nikki worried about what she called the aimlessness of many young people. She said, "[They] have nothing to do and then finding negative things to do with those who have nothing better to do." Faith reacted to this discussion of aimlessness with frustration. "But the things that there are to do, a lot of parents can't afford it. They're like 'put your kids in this,' 'put your kids in that,' but the person ain't getting no public assistance . . . and therefore you can't afford a lot of stuff to keep your kids occupied . . . or you're going to be working two jobs, that's with leaving your kids with a babysitter."

The undercurrent of these women's spatiality is the daily threat of violence and how to navigate their neighborhood to avoid it. Rosalind Harris (2005) provides a bold and theoretically rich analysis linking the historical forms of violence visited on the African American community and the contemporary forms of violence that plague the community. In articulating historical violence, Harris chronicles the changing forms of violence African Americans have endured, from the perpetuation of physical violence upon enslaved African Americans, to the structural forms of violence imposed through institutional racism post-Emancipation, to the symbolic violence in Black stereotypes of inferiority and sexual promiscuity, to contemporary forms of state violence and police surveillance that target young Black youth in the nation's War on Drug efforts. These macro-perspective forms of violence—physical, structural, symbolic, and state—have a direct link to the high rates of violence from drug and gang activity in the inner city today. While Harris's work is geared toward mental health professionals, I find her unique characterization of Black women and children as "witnesses" to be particularly meaningful. She writes:

> Violence in the forms of whippings, lynchings, murder, rape, and other forms of sexual violence by African American and White men are all part of the historical experience of African American women. In addition, African American women have borne witness to the violence experienced by their children throughout history. Today they are witnesses and victims of a substantial amount of violence within their communities and within their homes. They are also perpetrators of violence within these respective spheres. Exposure to violence as witnesses has taken the forms of witnessing beatings, muggings, and murders resulting from stabbing and shooting. Research indicates that this exposure to violence is both frequent and severe, with 100% of African American women in one study reporting that they both witnessed and experienced violence. (Harris 2005, 180–81)

Harris goes so far as to equate such pervasive witnessing of violence to the experience of people who live in war zones and the resulting symptoms of this prolonged exposure to violence with posttraumatic stress disorder. She criticizes current policies and programs that seek solutions to curb street violence in inner cities without the concomitant understanding of structural violence:

> To date, federal, state, and local policies have not been shaped to respond to conditions within the inner cities as if they were indeed war zones. Violence by and large continues to be conceptualized as an individual-level phenomenon preventable and treatable through law enforcement, the courts, and medical establishments. The underlying causes of chronic community violence (i.e., eroded economies and social networks with resulting poverty and social alienation) are left unacknowledged and unaddressed. (Harris 2005, 184)

What can we ascertain about the relationship between the environment and well-being? Gayle Phillips (1996) addresses the relationship between housing quality and stress more directly. Stress serves as the intervening variable between housing quality and neighborhood satisfaction.

Using the data from the National Survey of Black Americans, she questions which specific concerns about housing and neighborhood influence stress and neighborhood satisfaction. She divides the categories of housing and neighborhood concerns into subjective social indicators, objective social indicators, personal attributes of the respondents to the survey, and location of residence of the respondent. Subjective social indicators included eleven variables that measure the respondents' perceptions of their community.

The three strong factors that emerge from her analysis are neighborhood crime-police relations, neighborhood services, and neighborhood social relations. Neighborhood crime-police relations are an index of responses associated with police satisfaction, crime problems, and the perception of the relations between the local enforcement and the neighbors. Her findings indicate that stress is a critical variable in explaining neighborhood satisfaction, and that the housing and neighborhood concerns that factor in stress vary among Black men and Black women. For women in the study, the concerns that were most significant include neighborhood crime-police relations.

Amy Schulz et al. (2000) also expand on the relationship between neighborhood context and psychological distress. Researchers point to the history of racial segregation and economic divestment of the city of Detroit to support their research agenda, which rests on the notion that psychological distress and life satisfaction are related to community's economic context. To understand the community context for life satisfaction and psychological distress, the researchers divided the respondents by economic status. The high poverty group included respondents who lived in census tracts where 20 percent or more of the household's incomes were below the poverty line. The low poverty group of respondents lived in tracts where there were fewer households whose income were below the poverty line. Seventy-two percent of the African Americans and 11 percent of whites from the study sample constituted the high poverty group.

Regardless of residence within high or low poverty areas, Blacks in the sample reported more exposure to events they interpreted as unfair treatment. Researchers subdivided the construct of unfair treatment into measures of temporality: the first measure of unfair treatment is called "everyday" discrimination that occurred within the last year. The second measure for unfair treatment is called "acute," biased events that occurred over the respondent's lifetime. They concluded that, while there were higher levels of psychological distress reported by African Americans, these findings were not as significant when they divided the groups by poverty rather than race. In other words, psychological distress is quite complex, involving both elements of race and poverty. They conclude that, "like psychological distress, racial differences in life satisfaction in the Detroit metropolitan area appear to be influenced by the concentration of African Americans in census tracts with high levels of poverty" (Schulz et al. 2000, 327).

Christine Bevc et al. (2005) take a decidedly classic perspective on environmental justice in the relationship between neighborhood risk and psychological well-being in their study on the residents living near the Wingate Road Municipal Incinerator Dumpsite in Fort Lauderdale, Florida, which had been listed as a significant source of pollution by the Environmental Protection Agency in 1989. The Bevc et al. study distinguishes itself among environmental justice literature, because it tests not only the relationship between people and environmental exposure, but also the link between exposure and psychological well-being. Psychological well-being was measured using the Impact of Events Scale (IES), which determined the extent of intrusive stress and stress avoidance, and the Depression Scale, which measured the extent of depression.

They found that the female respondents reported higher levels of stress avoidance than the males surveyed. They point to evidence in the literature that women's heightened sense of environmental risk associated with toxins in the environment is the result of their greater concern about the health of their families. So the gendered dimension of stress avoidance researchers discovered is attributed to the notion that female respondents use stress avoidance as a coping mechanism.

Robert Jones and Shirley Rainey (2006) look at the racial differences in environmental concern among predominantly African American residents of the Red River Community and other Clarksville residents in Tennessee. The Red River Community has the highest rates of poverty in the Clarksville area and is also host to problems associated with urban blight: decaying infrastructure, abandoned housing, and vacant lots. After conducting interviews and mailed surveys, the researchers found that Blacks were more concerned than their white neighbors about environmental quality, most notably abandoned buildings and vacant lots, as well as water quality. Blacks were more likely to relate poor environmental quality to adverse health impacts. Moreover, Blacks were more likely to perceive a failure of local government to deal with such issues. The authors conclude that perceptions of environmental risks are shaped by race and socioeconomic status (SES). This study is perhaps most significant in its broad view of environmental injustice. While the Red River Community is a classic environmental justice case study, given its socio-demographics and exposure to water pollution and municipal waste dump, the authors also include urban blight and decay as environmental hazards. Most environmental justice analyses focus on more acute forms of environmental hazards, such as industrial-sized waste generators, incinerators, and dumps. Jones and Rainey's work represents an interesting expansion of the idea of environmental hazards.

Diane R. Brown (2003) offers a conceptual model of Black women's mental health in her edited volume entitled *In and Out of Our Right Minds: The Mental Health of African American Women.* She posits that racism and sexism are inextricably tied to Black women's socioeconomic status and that the triangulation of these three elements combines to affect the overall mental well-being of Black women. The mediating factors of race, gender, SES, and mental well-being include social and psychological stressors, compromised physical health, and changes in health behaviors. Brown pays particular attention to the multiple roles that Black women must juggle that lead to chronic stress. They are more likely to live in inner cities and in segregated neighborhoods and may be exposed to environmental conditions that characterize those neighborhoods, such as lead poisoning, pest infestation, and decaying residences and infrastructure, along with air and noise pollution. However, there are counteracting positive forces in Black women's lives that contribute to higher rates of well-being, as I will reveal in the next chapter on the Photovoice portion of the South

Side mothers project. Examples of elements that strengthen Black women's resilience include reliance on religion and the strength of extended families and other social networks. The next chapter illustrates this: although the mothers presented a number of photos that highlighted the urban decay of abandoned homes and crowded storefronts, they also captured poignant pictures of faith and family.

5

Women's Photovoice from Belfast to the South Side

This is what I wrote for this picture. This photo is of my two sons on my stairs. The gate you see is a security gate. It gets locked at night to stop unwanted visitors . . . from harmin' my family when we are in bed. Most families, mostly 90% of the families in the community have some sort of security in their homes. The children in the community are used to this. Mine have never asked why we have this and we will never remove this gate as I do not trust enough yet . . . When I go to bed and know it's locked, I sleep. If I hadn't got them, my nerves would be shot.

   —"Jacqueline" in Alice McIntyre, "Through the Eyes of Women"

This is a picture of an abandoned house across from my home, and it's been like this for years. I just wonder when they're going to fix it up . . . they go around fixin' a whole lot of other stuff, and I was like, it's right here every day when I come outside—it's the first thing I see. And I just call it "the Homeless House" cause it's the house that nobody fixes up.

   —Faith describing her photo "First Thing I See" in the Syracuse
   Community Mapping and Health Photovoice Project

The quotes above appear in separate Photovoice projects in two different countries. The first is from Jacqueline, a mother living near Monument Road, a community in Belfast, Northern Ireland. The second is from Faith, a young mom living in Syracuse. There is an unlikely connection between the mothers on the South Side of Syracuse and those in Belfast. Both groups of mothers try to keep their families safe and healthy in the midst of violent neighborhoods. In her article, "Through the Eyes of Women," Alice McIntyre (2003) chronicles her use of Photovoice in Monument Road, which underwent thirty years of sectarian violence between various factions in Ireland and the British government. When I first ran across the article, I wasn't aware of the parallels between these working-class European women and the women of color in an impoverished U.S. neighborhood. But both of their neighborhoods are plagued with random violence and the mothers must deal with daily stress related to their complete lack of power over their family's security. As I do in my work, McIntyre attempts to draw a line between the mother's identity and the impact of the neighborhood in which she dwells. She found that Photovoice was not only useful in exploring the daily lives of the Monument Road mothers but also that the process of capturing and sharing their images created an engaging and supportive environment among the women. As such, Photovoice serves as a valuable tool in feminist methodology.

The previous chapter on community mapping reveals that, despite the threat of violence, the South Side mothers engage in place making by relying on the stable institutions within the neighborhood and find comfort in the myriad of green spaces within the community. Photovoice expands on these themes of safety, health, and environment. I agree with McIntyre that Photovoice is a highly useful methodological tool that complements the tenets of feminist theory. I also contend that Black feminist theory is also a useful paradigm for interpreting the images that African American mothers captured through the Photovoice exercise, because women are allowed to clearly articulate their points of view through the lens of a camera. Their images shed light on the world they inhabit, highlight the relationships that are important to them, and provide a sharper focus on the threats to their well-being that other research methodologies cannot.

Photovoice is the brainchild of Caroline Wang and Mary Ann Burris, who first used it as a participatory action project with women in rural China in 1994. Since then, numerous researchers have employed Photovoice methodology. While the social location of Photovoice participants may vary, all are typically from marginalized groups in society: youth (Brazg et al. 2011; Strack et al. 2004; Streng et al. 2004; Tanjasiri et al 2011; Wang et al. 2004), low-income residents (Nowell et al. 2006; Stevens

2010), women (Cornwall et al 2010; McIntyre 2003; Wang et al. 1998), the homeless (Bukowski and Buetow 2011; Wang et al. 2000), older people (Baker and Wang 2006; Mahmood et al. 2012; Novek et al 2012; Rosen et al. 2011; Rush et al. 2012), those with HIV and AIDS (Hergenrather et al. 2006; International Visual Methodologies for Social Change Project n.d.), rural residents (Neill et al. 2011) and the mentally challenged (Booth and Booth 2003; Woolrych 2004).

The underlying principle that guides this type of research is the value of experiential knowledge. In the face of research methodologies, both qualitative and quantitative, that position the researchers' and social scientists' perspective as the most important, Photovoice distinguishes itself as an approach that democratizes knowledge. Originally termed *photo novella* by Wang and Burris (1994), it was designed to bring new, local voices to public policy decision making. While the researcher may choose the theme of the Photovoice project, participants are usually given latitude in interpreting those themes. In regard to research protocol, Photovoice generally involves a series of sessions where participants receive cameras and later return to discuss selected images. Some groups meet for a few weeks to a few months. Some pictures are captured on disposable cameras; others use inexpensive 35mm cameras. Despite these variations, Photovoice projects share the purpose of highlighting the everyday lives of their participants. One key outcome of each project is a final community exhibition of selected participant pictures.

Wang (1999) considers the theoretical underpinnings of Photovoice to be empowerment education, documentary production, and feminist theory. *Empowerment education* refers to the ideas espoused by Brazilian educator and activist Paolo Freire (2002) and his approach to teaching literacy and political education among rural farmers in his native country. In his seminal work, *Pedagogy of the Oppressed*, Freire contends that liberation from oppression begins with the development of a critical consciousness: unveiling the systems of hierarchy and privilege that lead to inequity in society, while reimagining a world with humanity for all. He warns that, without the critical consciousness, the oppressed would only succeed in modeling their oppressors. Integral to Freire's pedagogy is the element of *praxis,* which he defines as "reflection and action upon the world in order to transform it" (Freire 2002, 36). Examples of the Freirian teaching approach include *problem posing* and the *teacher as mediator*. Expanding on the ideas of critical consciousness and praxis, the Freirian method poses questions to the students about their world, particularly its disadvantages. Out of this discussion participants gain a greater awareness of their reality and, more specifically, an increased literacy. The idea of the teacher as mediator is based on an ideological commitment to flattening hierarchies, starting with the classroom. Freire rejects the idea of teachers as expert and leader but promotes their role as mediator, with a mutually beneficial relationship between instructor and students. Photovoice borrows Freirian principles of praxis (reflection), problem posing, and the researcher as mediator rather than expert. According to Wang and Burris, "In Freirian terms, photographs serve as one kind of 'code' that reflects the community back upon itself, mirroring the everyday social and political realities that influence people's lives. In photo novella, the women's images and words form the curriculum" (1994, 172).

Some of the most iconic images have been captured by documentary photographers and photojournalists. My most vivid media news images are the 1972 image "The Girl in the Picture," of the young Kim Phuc running naked down the road in the aftermath of a napalm attack, 1985's "Afghan Girl," whose haunted green eyes are unforgettable, and the poignant photo of the firemen cradling a dying toddler from the rubble of the Oklahoma City bombing. Can you imagine a scenario where those behind the lens were members of the community rather than journalists? Documentary photography has struggled with the critique about unequal power relations between photographers and their subjects. There is a similar conversation among progressive social scientists about the uneven relationship between researchers and their subjects. Photovoice methodology arises out of this conversation and seeks to balance those relationships, between photographer and subject, between researcher and subject, by shifting the power to the subjects or community members. They dictate what's being photographed, and the researcher facilitates discussion around those photographs.

Returning to the purpose of McIntyre's work in Belfast, she argued that the community participatory nature of the Photovoice project dovetails with feminist practices. Wang and Burris (1994) also write broadly of feminist principles within its methodology. The assumptions and goals of Photovoice complement the epistemologies underlined by Black feminism. Wang and Burris point to Rhoda Linton's essay, "Toward a Feminist Research Method" (1990) for the specific ways in which Photovoice complements feminist study. I would add the work of Deborah King in her essay "Multiple Jeopardy, Multiple Consciousness: The Context of a Black Feminist Ideology" (1988) to highlight the ways in which the goals of Photovoice and the tenets of Black feminist theory are enmeshed. King identifies four principles of Black feminism. First, this ideology declares the visibility of Black women and acknowledges the special status of occupying positions of both Black and female. Second, Black feminism asserts self-determination as essential, allowing Black women the right to interpret and define their experiences. Third, it challenges the system of multiple oppressions (racism, sexism, classism) that exist within society and within social movements that promote civil rights and women's rights. Finally, Black feminist ideology presumes Black women's agency as strong and independent subjects, not merely victims of multiple oppressions.

Despite the relation of Photovoice to feminism and its obvious complement to the principles of Black feminism, only a handful of Photovoice projects have focused on Black female subjects exclusively. Notable mentions include collaboration between Killion and Wang (2000), Lopez et al. (2005), and Washington and Moxley (2008). Cheryl Killion and Caroline Wang explore the intergenerational link between young Black women and Black female elders in a Photovoice project. Over a six-month period, two young, Black, homeless mothers met with three Black female seniors to discuss their photography relating to their housing situation. Discussions were structured around three key questions: (1) What are the things/places that I love; (2) what are the things (people, places, events, situations) that have an impact on my life; and (3) what do we (Photovoice group) have in common? Despite differences in age and living situations, the women found that there were commonalities. This project touched on themes of space and place that are central to the South Side Photovoice project. The authors write that "the women expressed the significance of space and place for developing and retaining family rituals and traditions" (Killion and Wang 2000, 314). Moreover, this work illustrated the multiplicative effects of racism, sexism, and classism in relation to claiming space and place: "Two challenges of being African American, female, poor, and a mother came to light: finding affordable, suitable housing, and raising children with limited resources" (Killion and Wang 2000, 318). Other themes that emerged included my own space, my own place, transitions, kinships/friendships, our heritage, our hope, children are a blessing, and the perils of poverty. Unlike other Photovoice projects, there was no exhibition at the end of the workshop period. However, the strong bonds the women formed during the project led to continued relationships even after it ended. The authors point out that the Photovoice process enabled participants to engage in "shared lives;" taking photographs and providing stories related to those images. The issues of home and children and struggle were salient within the group.

While the work presented by Olivia Washington and David Moxley (2008) does not fit neatly within the bounds of Photovoice methodology, their innovative use of visualization and performances around Black women's lives places it within the context of the other work presented in this chapter. The authors note, "What began as a project focused almost exclusively on therapeutic intervention in 2001 evolved by 2005 in an expanded project of therapeutic support and social action informed by the narrative content of the lived experience of homelessness among the participants" (Washington & Moxley, 2008, 160). The aims of their project were twofold: engage older African American homeless women in an intervention designed for a transition out of homelessness while incorporating humanist methods into social research.

The project entitled "Telling My Story" relied upon the use of photography, interviews, narratives, a collaborative quilt, and other artifacts. Eight women in the Detroit area participated. The project culminated in a public exhibition and education forum. Unlike conventional Photovoice methodology, the photographs were produced by an artist who worked under the direction of the eight participants. Each participant collaborated in the production of a conceptual portrait of herself:

The piece itself does not merely present an object, but it communicates a critique or commentary on homelessness, in which the lived experience, captured through the purposeful arrangement of artifacts, is seen through the eyes of a real person. That the person is standing next to the portrait gives the concept even more power . . . The conceptual portraits align elements of plight and efficacy as the women identify representations of the social forces that brought them into homelessness and their emergence out of homelessness, typically portrayed as an effort of personal triumph. (Washington & Moxley, 2008, 161)

The city of Detroit is an important backdrop to the narrative of the homeless women in the exhibition. Washington and Moxley conclude that Detroit, an oppressive space, is in a transition similar to the participants. As such, the presentation becomes a mix of landscapes of hope and promise. Homeless shelters and other social services are located within environmentally degraded parts of this postindustrial city, adding to the terrain of abandoned housing and urban decay. Ultimately, the exhibition and work in "Telling My Story" highlights the women's agency, how each was able to transition from life on the streets to reclaim a place of her own.

Ellen Lopez et al. (2005) present the results of the Inspirational Images Project, a Photovoice exercise among thirteen African American breast cancer survivors in rural North Carolina. The project was designed with three key purposes. The first was to engage survivors in investigating how their quality of life may be impacted by racial status and rural background. Second, after the initial investigation, the researchers sought to develop a conceptual framework of quality of life that incorporated the impacts of race and other social and cultural variables. Finally, the project was intended to promote social action by engaging local leadership in developing culturally sensitive medical interventions.

The Lopez et al. article also evaluates the effectiveness of Photovoice in initiating a community-based, participatory action project. As such, the authors paid a good deal of attention to reflection. Participants were asked, "How did you feel using the camera? How did you go about asking people if you could take their picture? How enjoyable was it for you to complete your photo-assignment? What suggestions do you have for improving the project?" (Lopez et al. 2005, 331). They conducted five photo-discussion sessions over a seven-month period, with participants defining their own photo assignments and assisting in clarifying concepts and themes that arose from the group discussions. The participants understood that they were not only the photographers but also an integral part of the research team. A conceptual framework arose out of the project that highlighted four quality-of-life concerns for rural African American breast cancer survivors: finding support, adjusting to the idea of being a survivor, finding comfort with the future, and serving as role models. The participants invited guests, called "influential advocates," to attend a special forum for their photo exhibition. Strategies were presented and prioritized during the course of the forum. Later project participants and their influential advocates volunteered to serve on task forces that arose from those priorities.

Black women as subjects in the previous research examples are not happenstance. These researchers recognize that Black women, given their social location, are uniquely vulnerable in their struggles to obtaining affordable housing, health care for chronic disease, and other social ills. Race and gender are not treated as variables. Rather, these researchers acknowledge that race, gender, and oftentimes class are organizing principles within social life. This commitment to place Black women and their experiences at the center of the analysis is central to Black feminist epistemology. The protocol around the creation of Photovoice methodology adheres to this epistemology.

Photovoice in Syracuse

The South Side Photovoice project adopted many of the aforementioned principles of Photovoice methodology: lessons in photography basics and ethics, informed consent and participants' ownership of copyright, weekly sessions discussing participants' images, and a community exhibition at the project's conclusion. We began the Photovoice portion of the South Side project at the second Saturday workshop. This workshop taught basic photographic principles to the participants, distributed the digital camera kits, and introduced the women to the Syracuse University campus. Recall that the first workshop on community mapping was held in the South Side at the local public health center. I decided to bring the women to the African American Studies Department. Later, we visited the on-campus community darkrooms, a public access photography and digital imaging studio. Law school professor and photographer Paula Johnson agreed to give the mothers the photography workshop. After the tutorial, I covered the responsibilities and ethics of taking images of people and distributed consent forms for those featured in the photos to sign. I also initiated some role-playing exercises to stress the importance of safety when taking photos. We discussed scenarios when it might not be safe to take pictures, such as during drug deals or other criminal activity. After the group had lunch, they walked to the darkrooms for a short tour of the facilities and to receive their camera kits.

I arrived at the darkrooms a few minutes after the group did. When I got there, I noticed that some of the women were visibly upset. They told me that, during the three-hundred-yard walk from lunch to the darkrooms, a campus security officer confronted the group. Even after they explained their purpose on campus, the officer proceeded to personally escort them to the darkrooms. They said the officer was dubious about their presence on campus. I was appalled. This incident demonstrated the invisible but pervasive divisions of privilege between the university and the South Side community. Moreover, it vividly illustrated the impact of the highly surveilled space that exists to maintain those divisions. The Black women's bodies were marked as outsiders on the predominantly white, private college campus. Their presence as a group branded them as interlopers, and campus security was quick to respond. The incident was quietly put to rest as the darkroom employee highlighted the features of the computer lab, but I'm sure that none of us would forget it.

After the tour, each woman received a digital camera, memory card, and camera bag. I told them to take as many images as they wanted. I soon realized that the cameras drained batteries quickly, however. So the following week, each woman was given a set of rechargeable batteries and a small portable charger. For the last two workshops, the group returned to the conference room of the South Side health center. To accommodate schedules, I offered two Saturday sessions: Session A was scheduled to start at 10 a.m. and end at 1 p.m. and Session B was scheduled from 3 to 6 p.m., with lunch served between those sessions. The women were invited to attend either session, based on their personal schedules.

Three sets of data in the form of photographs resulted from the Photovoice sessions during the last two weeks of June: (1) each participant's photo album of images taken in that two-week period, (2) images selected for Photovoice discussion, and (3) finally, those images that were ultimately chosen for the community exhibition at the end of the project.

At the beginning of each workshop, participants gave me permission to download all the photos that they had taken during the week. This download represents each participant's photo album. In the first week after she received her camera, Makeba took more than a hundred pictures!

The second dataset of photographs critical to my analysis are the six photos that each woman chose from all of her weekly pictures. Continuing the theme set by the mapping exercise, I asked each participant to choose three pictures that represented positive, safe, and healthy aspects of her life on the South Side and three that represented negative, unsafe, and unhealthy aspects of her community. Not every woman chose six pictures to present. There were 135 total pictures presented during the workshops.

The third and final dataset of photos were the thirty-seven photos that participants chose to enlarge, frame, and display at the community exhibition.

The Photo Albums

Makeba produced the largest dataset of images taken over the course of the project: 193. She was followed by Nina (145) and Faith (134). The other women averaged approximately twenty-five images each over the course of the workshops. Unlike other Photovoice projects, the women's instructions were broad: go out and take pictures of your community, both negative and positive. The images ran the gamut from self-portraits and those featuring children or adults to scenes that represented violence, nature, or the built environment. The digital cameras had a video camera feature that some of the participants took advantage of. The cameras also had special-effects commands that would convert images into sepia tone, black and white, graphic frame, and text placement. Some of these features were explored. Faith was perhaps the most creative in presenting sepia-toned and black-and-white images.

Recall the purpose of this project: to establish links between space and identity as it is informed by poor and working-class African American mothers in an urban environment. Although I was most concerned with the impacts of environmental degradation as it related to the Midland Avenue wastewater treatment facility, the latest environmental hazard in the South Side, or other signs of urban decay, I did not want to overemphasize the environment. This project was more exploratory. My primary goal was to understand how these women conceptualized their environment. The community mapping exercise set the spatial context for viewing the community as a whole. After exploring how they defined environment, I needed to establish what for them constituted positive and negative elements of that environment. It is important to note that these workshops took place during a time of great pride in the South Side community: the annual Juneteenth celebration. Paradoxically, these weeks were marred by a spike in violence within the community. Without a doubt, these two poles of experience—cultural pride and grief—influenced the participants during this period. It was within these spatial and temporal contexts that the South Side mothers used the cameras in an attempt to document their lives.

Image Coding and Analysis

Although the photo albums were the largest source of visual data for the project, the second dataset of images was the most comprehensive. These were the photographs that each participant presented and wrote captions for. The sessions where participants presented their photos were recorded and transcribed. My analysis is based primarily on the presentation pictures that comprised the second dataset. Analysis includes three key stages for theme development in the photos presented: coding, blind testing, and recoding. This iterative coding process was influenced by the Photovoice evaluation project by Foster-Fishman et al. (2005). This research team interviewed sixteen youth and adult Photovoice participants to determine the project's impact. All five of the article's authors read the transcripts of the interviews independently to identify themes and coding schema. They came together to identify patterns in the coding and then finalized a coding framework to use throughout the rest of the data analysis.

The first stage of the South Side Photovoice project coding involved my review of the 135 images presented at the workshops. I assigned the images identification codes that represented the photographer's initials, the number of the Photovoice session (first or second), the number of the photo in the order of its presentation, and the total number of pictures presented by the photographer during the course of the workshop. The actual photographs and transcripts were labeled with the initials of the participants' real names. During the analysis process I assigned the women their pseudonyms. For example, the code "HT2-1-5" meant that the image was taken by Harriet, and it was the first photo presented out of a total of five images that she showed during the second workshop. Next, photos were divided into broad categories based on a combination of their captions and the image itself ("children," "playground," "work," etc.). After this initial sorting, the following categories emerged: people, structures/ built environment, and natural environment. The category *people* includes images where the main focus was on models, both children and adults. Photos in the category of *structures/built environment* typically featured both residential and nonresidential buildings. Finally, *natural environment* represented landscapes or streetscapes with no discernible primary residence or building.

Next, the photographs were sorted again to further refine the categories. Here's where the strength of Photovoice methodology comes into the analysis. As a researcher, I have both the images and the participants' captions for them, as well as their detailed descriptions of the image as evidence for my coding themes. For example, Nikki presented a photo of an empty playground on a sunny day. She decided to give it the caption, "Where Are the Children?" What initially appeared to be a neutral image of a playground became infused with a negative connotation. Then, imagine that that image and caption are accompanied by the photographer's voice in an audio transcript, explaining that an empty playground is an unsafe playground because of the area where it is located.

The category *people* was refined to differentiate between images that featured adults versus those that featured children. I also highlighted and separated photos that were self-portraits or pictures of the participants as a group ("self") and adults who were identified as being mentors or those that

they turned to for support ("mentor"). Two group photographs of the participants were presented during the workshops. Two different participants took
them shortly after the women received their cameras at the community
darkrooms. During this second sorting, I divided the category *structures/
built* environment into two subcategories: institutions and houses. Photos
in *institutions* typically featured the nonresidential built environment: community centers, churches, and other public buildings. Images under *houses*
were residential dwellings. I left the last category, *natural environment*,
unchanged in the second round of coding. After both rounds of sorting
and coding, it was time to check the strength of my coding categories.

To test the reliability of these themes, I asked three people unfamiliar
with the project to look at all of the pictures produced by the Photovoice
exercises and come up with possible categories. These coders did not have
access to the transcripts related to the project, only to the captions for
each picture. They did not know what the participants looked like, so they
did not recognize images of the participants.

The first independent coder yielded similar broad themes of children, nature, and housing. She suggested fourteen categories, more coding
schemes that I originally developed. She divided the images of children
into two subcategories by age: infants and toddlers were separated from
school-aged children. The coder created the theme *city issues*, when sorting the photos that hinted of criminality. She also divided images into
categories by gender: female-dominated and male-dominated images.
She further subdivided the institutions into help organizations, places of
worship, and recreational facilities. The most notable departure from my
original categories were three photos that the coder grouped as subjects
depicting mourning and memorial. Zora's photo entitled "Another Life
Taken" captures a street memorial, typically the site of a murder, memorial-
ized with makeshift wreaths, flowers, candles, and stuffed toys. The second
street mourning/memorial photo, called "Death Knocking on Your Back
Door," was taken by Nikki. Finally, Makeba's photo "Life Is Short" depicted
a funeral program from a recently murdered relative.

The second independent coder featured a similar theme, which he
labeled *memory and remembrance*. Coders numbers two and three had significantly fewer categories in their blind coding than number one, nine

and seven categories respectively. Other similar categories between coder #1 and coder #2 were for recreation, abandoned/uninhabitable housing, and charitable organizations. Coder #3 designated a category for urban art. All the testers created the theme of children. Coder #2 did not create a category for men but did designate one for women. Overall, the coding by unbiased testers seems to reaffirm my coding themes: *children, adults, mentors, institutions, housing,* and *environment.* After testing, I decided to add another category to my original coding scheme: *memorial.* These themes represent patterns for the images in terms of frequency. However, it is also important to note the outliers, those themes that were not numerous but revealing just the same for their distinctiveness. These honorable mentions include the role of males in the images and representations of black fatherhood.

Overall, analysis of the project's Photovoice images indicates a fairly balanced view of the community. Themes that show positive aspects of the community centered on the notion of children representing the future, the importance of mentorship and support, nature, and the importance of social institutions like churches and schools. Negative themes emphasized gang and drug violence and the ugliness of abandoned housing. In fact, the women took at least eight photos of abandoned housing in their neighborhood. These themes were also echoed in other Photovoice projects with mothers as subjects, such as McIntyre's (2003) work with Belfast mothers and Killion and Wang's (2000) Photovoice project with African American mothers. The following section details those themes and compares my findings with those in McIntyre's work and in Killion and Wang's project.

Children

Nearly a quarter of all of the images produced by the South Side moms featured children, usually their own children or grandchildren and young relatives. Similar themes were found among the African American women in Killion and Wang's Photovoice project, especially the themes *friendship/kinship* and *children are a blessing.* In their results, Killion and Wang write: "An overwhelming number of the photographs showed the extent to which children were valued. The women's interpretations of their photographs revealed delight in children simply for their own sakes" (2000, 318).

All of the South Side moms presented at least one photograph of their children during the Photovoice discussions. Children are also a recurring theme in a number of images presented by Faith. She introduced the group to her son in a photo entitled "Needle in a Haystack." He's smiling directly into the camera, proudly balanced on his skateboard in a grassy area: "I took this picture because he be playing around with the skateboard when he's at my mom's house, so I call him my little black skateboarder, 'cause you don't see a lot of Black kids rolling around on skateboards. So I labeled this one, 'Needle in a Haystack' 'cause out of the skateboarders, you probably find like one or two of them that are black." Faith also took a picture of herself and her son, where she used the camera's graphic capabilities to draw a cartoon heart around them with the words "I Love You." Her caption was "Single Black Mom." She also presents children in her picture "Unity" and in a photo entitled "Black Beauty," which is an artful black-and-white image of a boy huddled beneath a towel after playing in a pool. In "Unity" she attempts to capture the inclusiveness of her family: "This one, I put as one of my positive pictures. My little cousin is here, and I like this one because I got a lot of different family members with disabilities, like the children, and I just like to see all of the kids, even if they are disabled, playing with the rest of the kids." Faith even captured a picture of Shirley's granddaughter in "Precious Moments" (see Figure 5.1).

Figure 5.1 is really a picture within a picture: Faith took a picture of Shirley's fingers grasping the camera and focused on her smiling grand-daughter when the red eye of the flash caught her eye. This picture was taken shortly after the women received their cameras at the community darkrooms studio on campus. Shirley's granddaughter is a natural model; she is smiling directly at the camera, with her head slightly tilted.

Like Faith, CJ's photos focused mainly on her children and grandchildren. She presented "Curiosity," a comic image of her infant granddaughter mesmerized by a television remote. She chose to feature this image in the community exhibition. Other pictures that portrayed her children and grandchildren were "Destiny," which shows her daughter, "Inquisitive" featuring her son, "Grandma's Little Helper" with her grandchild, "Baby Teaching Baby" with her daughter and grandchild and "Bathtime" with daughter and grandchild.

5.1. "Precious Moments" *(top)*, "Isaiah the Superhero" *(bottom)*. Used with permission of Southside Photovoice Project Collection.

The mothers captured the innocence of their children playing, smiling, and sleeping. Makeba took a photo of her siblings and their friends running down a hill, which she captioned "Exercise." She included a couple of photos of her toddler. In "Moment in Thought," she interpreted her toddler's mood in the arms of her sister: "That's my sister going [down a slide] with my daughter . . . That's another reason I took this picture, it looks like she's reaching out to something or someone, so it looks good to me." She offered the group another photo of her slumbering daughter in an image she called "Peaceful Sleeping."

Elizabeth provided one of the most vivid and artful examples of the images of children in a photo of her son she called "Isaiah the Superhero" (Figure 5.1). He is dressed in Spider-Man pajamas, arms raised and looking straight into the camera. She noted that the Spider-Man costume was his favorite. His dark eyes stare straight into the camera, arms clasped above his head, lips slightly pursed as if to say, "Look at me." Nina captured her son in a creative way in a photo she named "Divine." The viewer cannot see his face, only the top of his head, showcasing the intricate details of his elaborately braided hair, an obvious source of pride. Shirley showed her pride in a picture of her teenage son in his graduation gown, in a picture she titled "Success."

Unlike the others, Billie did not offer photos of her own children but saw the promise in other people's babies. In doing so, she confronted her own limitations as a mother. In "A New Beginning," she mused, "This is my best friend's . . . granddaughter . . . I call her my niece, you know. Since she's been born we just—she helps us both stay clean, too. When our kids was little, we was using, so now we got another baby in our lives. She helps me stay clean, too." Like Billie, Zora did not present any pictures of her children. However, she captured a moment shared between Gwen and Shirley, interacting over Gwen's newborn, which she brought to the workshop less than a week after delivery in "My Memory."

Patricia Hill Collins offers useful analysis in understanding motherhood from an intersectional frame. She contextualizes Black mothers' experiences through racial, gender, and class oppression and differentiates them from conventional feminist writing about motherhood. To do so, she first employs the term *motherwork*: "I use the term 'motherwork' to soften the existing dichotomies in feminist theorizing about motherhood that posit rigid distinctions between private and public, family, and work, the individual and the collective, identity as individual autonomy, and identity growing from the collective self-determination of one's group. Racial ethnic women's mothering and work experiences occur at the boundaries demarking these dualities" (1998, 199). One clear difference between motherwork and conventional feminist ideas of motherhood is the overwhelming concern mothers of color have with the physical and emotional survival of their children. Mothers of color must actively engage their children on issues of structural oppression, conveying strategies on how to overcome those obstacles while simultaneously building self-esteem, racial identity, and cultural pride.

In her research on mothers in Northern Ireland, McIntyre refers to the McWilliams's (1995) concept *frozen watchfulness*: "a state of being where one has a sense of impending doom about what might happen to them, their families, and in particular, their children. This sixth sense about 'what might happen next' results in the women living with an underlying anxiety about where their children are and whether they are safe while 'hanging about the streets'" (McIntyre 2003, 59). In my study, this concept is best illustrated by Josephine's discussion when she presented a picture of her son she called "My Hope": "I have so many hopes and dreams for him. He's a good child, and I can't even say that he's in the streets. He's a very good, very good child . . . He's fourteen, and he doesn't have any positive role models. His father is there. His father is not there." Her comments reflect the conundrum of a mother attempting to valiantly raise and protect her child in a harsh and sometimes violent environment. Later, as she continued to describe the same picture, she demonstrated how she's always cognizant of that spatiality: "He's right about Hudson [Street], where the eleven-year-old got shot. So despite all that, he's not out there [in the streets]."

I've personally experienced this source of pride in regard to motherhood in the Black community. I had always been ambivalent about parenthood, given my own parents' divorce and the financial struggles that my mother and I endured as she tried to raise me and my brother, alone. By my mid-twenties, family members began to ask when I was having a child, rather than when I would be getting married. When I reached my thirties,

I became defensive about the subject. One day when I was dropping Faith off at her home, she gave me a quizzical look when I told her that I didn't have any biological children.

Four months after the conclusion of the Photovoice project, I finally reached that elusive rite of passage: I became pregnant. By the start of my second trimester, I was ordered to strict bed rest. I had a stillbirth delivery of a little girl in March 3, 2008. We named her Mannone. A year after the conclusion of the Photovoice project, I had to grapple with the conundrum that while I was now a mother, I was without a living child. I finally understood the fierce devotion of motherhood, albeit briefly.

Mentorship and Support

So, how did the mothers cope with life, vacillating between the poles of familial pride and the frozen watchfulness of violent activity? One of the most interesting results of this research for me was the importance they placed not only upon mentors and role models for their children but upon formal and informal adult mentors for themselves. I saw themes of mentorship and support in the images of the adults depicted in the mothers' photographs from the South Side Photovoice project.

As noted in the previous section, Josephine struggled with raising a son whose father who was in and out of his life. She acknowledged the mentors for her son and for herself in two of the images that she presented during the workshop: "Mother's Instinct" and "Positive Role Model." In the first photo, two smiling adolescent girls flank an older woman who smiles meekly at the camera, eyes averted. Josephine identified the woman as her mother-in-law, who has served as a constant influence in her life since the age of sixteen: "You know you wanna be grown, and you want to be out there doing whatever you wanna do. She always been the one to show me direction even though she's many times made me mad. I just wanna be like 'Oh, I'm not gonna speak to her,' but she's always been there for me and my children." Her photo "Positive Role Model" strikes a similar pose. A broadly smiling man has his arms around young boys on each side, with a third kneeling in the front. All are dressed in dress shirts and ties. Josephine's son stands to the man's right. She told the group that the man pictured is the vice principal of her son's former school: "These three young men . . . he mentored them . . . he took on that responsibility and still has been there for them even though he doesn't teach at their school. And all of them graduated from eighth grade, and none of them hang in the street. So, that's just a good picture to see—three young Black men [and] a positive role model."

Billie's work is distinguished by the number of adults she highlighted as mentors, particularly in her quest to remain sober. Her pictures, "Community Teacher," "Inspiration," "Sister Strong," and "Comfort Zone" all focus on a network of support that helped make her commitment to sobriety possible. She pointed out a sobriety counselor working in a local nonprofit in her photo "Community Teacher": "She was about to go in and start a class, and I stopped her in the hallway. 'Come here and let me take your picture.' But I should have taken it when she was doing her class. It would have been better." In "Inspiration," she said of an older man she met at a drug rehabilitation program, years ago: "And he's a very positive person in my life today, I took this picture at Juneteenth last week, and you see the chess pieces and the chess board down here in the corner right here. 'Cause he's a chess maniac. I took it because he's [impacted] my life and a whole lot of other people's lives . . . He's a big inspiration in my life." Billie also captured her boss, who directs a program with the same name as the title of the photo, "Sister Strong": "So that's why I picked her picture, 'cause she's my life; she's in recovery just like I am, so I try to stay around positive people so I can stay positive." She even counted the group of Photovoice mothers as part of the positive network that she has created for herself. She captured the group in a picture she titled "Comfort Zone." Josephine took a similar shot of the group in a picture she called "Successful."

Like Billie, Faith acknowledged formal mentors that helped her prepare for her General Education Diploma (GED) exam. Faith portrayed her GED instructor in her photo entitled "Education Motivation": "I love Miss Linda, she'll make you try." Recall that Faith was about to forgo taking her GED exam in order to accommodate the schedule of the first day of the workshop. After encouragement, she agreed to take the exam that day and arrived late for the workshop. Faith succeeded in obtaining her GED.

Nina presented a photograph of two neighbors she called "My Angels." They sit on a porch looking into the camera. She credited their influence in helping her cope with the murder of a family member: "They mean so much to me. They have really helped me. These two women, they still walk with me, and they're just good sisters to have around . . . No matter what's going on, they have time for me." She repeated the phrase, "they walk with me." The idea of people who "walk with her" is a subtle yet powerful metaphor of the mentor's role. The popular understanding of a mentor is one who is older, wiser, and more experienced who helps you navigate your career. Nina's concept is more inclusive: someone who has time for her and walks with her through a difficult journey of losing someone unexpectedly and violently. A mentor does not have to have specific expertise, nor does she need to lead. The most important requirements are having the compassion and grace to walk beside her. I like that.

Another aspect of Collin's concept of "motherwork" is the emphasis on work separation, rather than work isolation, which assumes a dichotomy between the public and private sphere. Unlike white, middle-class mothers, African American women have always participated in the labor force. As such, their concerns center on the impacts of prolonged separation from their children. Collins proposes that the African American cultural marker of extended kin networks is a response to the dilemmas posed by work separation. This reliance on relatives and close friends to assist in childcare is also referred in some texts as *othermothering*. Othermothering capitalizes on the strength and wisdom of other, usually older, Black women to serve as caretakers and influential figures in family life.

Kevin Roy (2004) describes the inner city as the result of an ecological process, plagued by racial segregation, economic restructuring, long-term unemployment, poor school systems, erosion of job networks, and gang activity and subsequent surveillance by law enforcement. Under this scenario, he theorizes the spatial perceptions of low-income, noncustodial Black fathers and how they come to rely on kin-work to support their role as fathers. While my analysis is limited to Black mothers, Roy's work is a recent attempt to theorize about the obstacles posed by parenting within an unstable urban space and the strategies that rely on kinship network to overcome those obstacles. Roy's research centers on forty Black fathers in Chicago. One of the essential strategies that helped them overcome their spatial disadvantage in parenting was the adoption of a three-block safe

space reserved for family interaction. This three-block safe space was usually co-managed with the paternal grandmothers. In fact, nearly half of the
men Roy interviewed lived with their extended kin, usually mothers and
grandmothers, and saw home as a safe space. Roy's findings point to the
importance not only of spatiality but also of kinship networks.

Most scholarship on kinship within the black community references
Carol Stack's classic book *"All Our Kin": Strategies for Survival in a Black
Community* (1975). It demonstrates how kinship networks serve as coping
strategies to deal with abject poverty. While she emphasizes the exchange
value of kinship networks, a reexamination of this work points to the
interplay of space and network relations. For instance, she discusses the
spatial network map of one couple in her study, Magnolia and Calvin,
whose network spans more than twenty-five people, from biological relatives to legal and common-law unions to close family friends, within a five-
mile area of their home in the Flats community in Chicago.

However, kin networks can be as limiting as they are supportive. The
folks in those networks can take as much as they give in support, thereby
exacting a high cost for participation when it is time to reciprocate. It is
reasonable to assume that there is a difference in the kinship networks in
the previously mentioned scholarship and the mentors that the South Side
mothers chose to highlight in their images. Silvia Dominguez and Celeste
Watkins (2003) refine the notion of kinship networks as those that help
low-income moms get by, offering social support to assure survival, and
those networks that help moms get ahead by providing the social leverage
for upward mobility. Using ethnographic interviews with ten low-income
African American and Latina mothers in Boston, they find that primary
networks were comprised of family, friends, male partners, and social service agencies. Departing from existing kinship literature, Dominguez and
Watkins recognize social service agencies as integral source of support.
Some of the nonprofit organizations' staff form close social ties with their
clients. For example, Billie's close relationship with her sobriety counselor
and her subsequent images of her mentors as presented during the Photovoice workshop provide evidence for Dominguez and Watkins' claims. The
women in their study relied on services from community centers and other
nonprofit aid agencies in the greater Boston area. In the case of the South

Side mothers, affinity for stable social institutions like churches and community centers was significant enough to be affirmed outside of the theme of mentorship and support.

Importance of Social Institutions
and the Impacts of the Built Environment

Along with the valuable mentorship and supportive networks, the women also relied on the positive influences of community institutions on the South Side. The community mapping exercise in chapter 4 highlighted the importance of churches, schools, and community centers that make up the built environment around the South Side neighborhood. In her work with mothers from Monument Road in Ireland, McIntyre (2003) identified the local community center as one of three key sites of place-making among the mothers. For them, the center offered both social and emotional support for local families. There are a few community centers that dot the South Side community, and the South Side mothers highlighted them in ways similar to their Belfast counterparts. Gwen presented photos of two separate community centers: the Southwest Community Center ("Southwest") and a small center called the Faith and Hope Community Center ("Faith and Hope"). Recall that the Southwest Center was a conflicted space for the South Side mothers in the community mapping exercise. It had the unique designation of both a positive and negative element within the community. After much discussion, the women agreed that the programs and staff of the center were exemplary, but the space outside was plagued with random violent encounters.

A recurring theme emerged regarding faith-based institutions in photographic depictions of spiritual practice. Harriet presented two images of the same church; one called "God's House" featured the exterior and "House of Worship" showed the interior. She proclaimed, "And every Sunday, I'm there faithfully. Every Sunday . . . I got a very blessed pastor that cares about, not only the church members, but cares about the community, too." Josephine presented a photograph of a recently renovated church she called "Rebirth." Shirley submitted an image of her church captioned "Safe Haven," as seen in Figure 5.2. Makeba offered a glimpse of her small church in "Growing Up."

Sometimes the faith-based images did not include the obvious, like a church, but the photo's meaning and intent were infused with spiritual life and practice. Examples included Elizabeth's photos "Lean on Me" and "God's Glory," along with other religious photos by Makeba and Harriet entitled "Celebration" and "Voice of Salvation," respectively.

At first glance, "Lean on Me" (Figure 5.2) is obscure; the images are blurred and the whole scene is cast in a strange orange glow caused by the setting sun. There are two figures in the center. One man, his head bowed and his image cast in profile, clutches the shoulder of another. The other, taller person is facing away from the camera, and his arm clasps the first man's side. It appears that the taller person is holding the other up, as though he is injured. However, Elizabeth was capturing the poignant scene of a recent prayer circle in the park. A South Side church organized the vigil in response to the spike in violence that summer. Her presentation to the group gave weight to the scene in the photo; without it, one might infer a less sacred event. Her next photo, "God's Glory," was also taken at the prayer vigil in Kirk Park. It depicts the sunset; the tops of the trees are in shadow and the cloudless sky turns orange as the sun descends toward the horizon. It's an ethereal picture.

Makeba's "Celebration" shows the choir at her aunt's church. She chose it because it portrayed both Black men and women singing together. Harriet presented another photo featuring a choir in her "Voice of Salvation." The choir features her nieces. She told the group how she became their guardian less than a year earlier: "I went back home in [New] Jersey and got them . . . When I used to go home to see how she [another guardian] did them, she kept them in the back, always kept them in the house. So me and my brother put our heads together, and went back home and got them 'cause my son is twenty-seven and he's in college. I'm a mother all over again for these kids, but it's all right."

Church has offered many poor Black women spiritual solace in a harsh world. While my Nana worked long hours during the weekdays in the uniform cleaning plant, she shined bright on Sunday mornings as she prepared for church. I can't recall if she wore a uniform or street clothes to work each day, but I can distinctly remember her Sunday ensembles: suit, matching handbag and shoes, gloves, and hats that she lovingly preserved

5.2. "Safe Haven" *(top)*, "Lean on Me" *(bottom)*. Used with permission of South-side Photovoice Project Collection.

in hat boxes in her closet. Nana was resplendent on Sunday mornings at church. She sat near the front and whooped and hollered and sang weekly, to my chagrin. I didn't like the noisiness of my family's call and response to the reverend. I recall my embarrassment, sandwiched between Nana, my mother, or my Aunt Niecey as they prayed and sang and cried. Church was a major influence on my family. My great-grandmother, Nana's mother, founded a church, the First Baptist Church of Marshall Heights. I've only passed the church a few times in my adult life, and I'm always humbled to see her name carved in the stone of the church sign, "founded by Earline Smith." One of Nana's sisters was a famous local gospel singer, and another was an evangelist. Shortly before my Aunt Niecey's death, she attended seminary and began to travel as an evangelist. Southern Baptist tradition formed the backdrop of my childhood.

Much of the literature on African American religiosity and its relationship with well-being hails from community psychologists and sociologists. One recent work was the Jennifer van Olphen et al. (2003) study on the religiosity of African American women in a low-income neighborhood in Detroit, using a methodology based on the principles of community-based participatory action research (CBPAR). Six hundred and seventy-nine African American women were interviewed by other community members trained to interview them for this baseline health assessment in 1996. The extent of their religiosity was measured in three ways: organizational, nonorganizational, and subjective religious involvement. To measure organizational religious involvement, the women were asked how often they attended religious services. To measure nonorganizational religious involvement, they asked about the frequency of prayer. Finally, to measure the degree upon which respondents participated in subjective religious involvement, they inquired about the importance of spirituality in daily living.

To test for the effect of social support through religious involvement, the researchers asked about the frequency of support by church leadership and other congregants. Those responses on the various forms of religiosity were weighed against the respondent's general health and chronic medical conditions—specifically asthma, arthritis, hypertension, diabetes, and depressive symptoms. Statistical analysis supported the hypothesis of the positive relationship between religiosity and health. Specifically, organizational, nonorganizational, and subjective religious involvements were significantly associated with mental and physical health. Moreover, there was a positive association between religious thought and behavior on overall general health, and an inverse relationship between religiosity and the reporting of depressive symptoms and chronic conditions.

What about the role of social support as a mediating affect between religiosity and mental and physical health? The study found that women who identified themselves as church members and those who attended church more frequently were also more likely to report more social support from others in their congregation. However, when social support was added to the statistical model of the relationship between religiosity and health, the statistical strength of religiosity was muted: the relationship between religion and church attendance and fewer depressive symptoms was reduced to nonsignificance, and there was also a simultaneous reduction in the "magnitude of the positive relationship between church attendance and self-rated general health" (van Olphen et al. 2003, 553). Their results indicate that religious involvement is a strong predictor of positive mental and physical health; however, within this simple model the stronger element is the impact of social ties and connections among the congregants. Religiosity serves as a protective factor in challenges to mental and physical health. The variables that serve as proxies to measure religiosity are quite diverse: from having faith or belief to prayer and meditation to bible study, among others. Another complicating factor in studying the relationship between religiosity and health is the mechanism by which religious thoughts and behaviors affect health and well-being. One mechanism supported by the literature is social support. African American women's reliance on spiritual support can be seen as an extension of kinship or mentorship highlighted in the previous section. Thus, the impact of participation in organized religious communities results in more social ties and interactions, which in turn may lead to the overall benefit in the receipt and exchange of materials, services, and information.

Amber N. Douglas et al. (2008) investigated the relationship between spiritual well-being and mental health, among other psychological and behavioral variables, in a sample of homeless women. They found that in

African American women in particular, there was an inverse relationship between spiritual well-being and anxiety and posttraumatic stress symptoms. They concluded that spirituality is a coping mechanism for African American homeless women in their sample.

A qualitative study by Anne Brodsky (2000) explored the influence of religious thoughts and behavior among ten African American single mothers in a poor, urban neighborhood in Washington, D.C. While only half of the mothers she interviewed identified themselves as members of a church, she determined a level of religiosity that goes beyond church attendance. She highlighted four mechanisms of religious influence: (1) religious settings and people, (2) internal and individual values, (3) behavior, and (4) protection and blessing. Inherent in her discussion about the first mechanism, religious settings and people, is the element of social support, both directly by way of friendship and support of the clergy leader and the congregation, or indirectly in the form of services like the church's food pantry. Brodsky's findings about direct and indirect social support from the religious community coincide with that of van Olphen et al. on African American women in Detroit. The second element, internal role of religion, refers to "private spirituality": the reliance upon faith practices outside of organized religious activities. Single moms in Brodsky's study noted daily prayers, spiritual guidance in parenting, and what might be referred to as an internal optimism produced by religious faith. The third mechanism, behavior, refers to the manner in which religion affects the women's behavior, particularly when it comes to active coping with living daily in a community plagued by violence. Finally, the last mechanism is the reliance upon religious beliefs as a form of protection and blessing in an otherwise violent and chaotic space. She describes this mechanism as the "balance of helplessness and hope" (2003, 214). Echoing the notion of women's sensitivity to space and place in violent neighborhoods in Jones's book, *Between Good and Ghetto*, Brodsky notes that these single mothers maintain their resilience in part by actively withdrawing from the negative influences they see in their neighborhoods. Religiosity aids in resilience.

Marino Bruce and Michael Thornton (2004) attempted to measure the interaction effects of race and gender on various factors related to perceptions of personal control and found that religious participation by

Black women in their sample was positively associated with personal control. They defined personal control as the belief that one has agency in one's social world. I understand how the relationship between religiosity and the belief in the omnipotence of a higher power can simultaneously increase one's sense of agency and belief in the ability to change life situations, while at the same time accepting a sort of divine determinism about one's place in life. Rosalind Harris (2005) briefly notes an inherent liberation ideology in African American religious observation that might tip the scales on the power of religiosity to promote individual agency versus diminishing it.

Perhaps there is no clearer example of this convergence of fierce religiosity combined with a fervent sense of social change in the African American tradition of liberation theology than in the life and times of one of my personal heroes, Fannie Lou Hamer. Born the youngest of twenty children of a Mississippi sharecropper in 1917, Fannie Lou Townsend only received a sixth-grade education, but became an instrumental figure in the mobilization of Black voting efforts in rural Mississippi in the turbulent 1960s. She is perhaps best known for her stance challenging the representation of the Mississippi Democrats during the 1964 National Democratic Convention in Atlantic City, New Jersey. Manning Marable and Leith Mullings reprinted her address to the 1971 NAACP Defense Fund Institute, where she describes her fight for civil rights in prophetic terms: "But we are not going to liberate ourselves. I think it's a responsibility. I think we're special people. God's children is going to help in the survival of this country if it's not too late" (2003, 420).

In my Photovoice study, CJ's photos offered new perspectives of social institutions and places of resources, beyond churches and community centers. She took a picture of a bank in "Possibilities" and the local welfare office in "Making Ends Meet." She selected "Making Ends Meet" for the community exhibition. She even chose a picture of our weekly meeting place, the neighborhood health center, in a picture she named "Community Well Being." Harriet showed the group a photo that she took on the grounds of Dr. Martin Luther King Elementary School in "I Have a Dream." Nikki rounded out the theme around positive social institutions with her snapshot of the exterior of the Salvation Army building in a photo entitled "Moving on Up." She acknowledged using its services when she was homeless.

Not all South Side institutions were portrayed positively. In fact, the mothers considered some of the built environment within the South Side as cultivating gang activity and violence. The theme that stood out prominently among their photographs of negative influences was the problem of abandoned housing. Some references were blatant, as in the title for Zora's photo taken on a grassy corner lot facing a house, which she captioned "Drug Infested." Shirley's photo of a boarded-up house near her home, partially obscured by overgrown bushes, was called "Fire Hazard" (Figure 5.3). Josephine's photo "Neglect" illustrated the close proximity of boarded houses to habitable residences. Her photo features a two-story home with windows boarded up on both levels and small "No Trespassing" signs flanking its front door. Toward the left of the photo, one can see that the neighboring house is inhabited. Its second-floor windows appear to have roller blinds. The fender of a black car can be seen in the lower left corner, more evidence that folks live right next door to such blight.

It was surprising that five photos representing negative built environment were given the same caption: "Too Close for Comfort," implying the mothers' caution with proximity to potential hazards. Nina gave three of her photos this caption, Shirley, one (see Figure 5.3), and Billie, one. Most of the photographs depicted abandoned housing, while the others showed a bar where a patron had been stabbed to death weeks earlier. Nina produced the most images of abandoned housing. In addition to the three called "Too Close for Comfort," she presented another called "Stop the Madness." She appeared visibly upset during the workshops when she discussed the photos of boarded homes near her own residence.

This chapter opened with Faith's comment about her close proximity to an abandoned house as shown in a photo she titled "First Thing I See" (Figure 5.4), which was the very first picture that Faith presented at the Photovoice workshop. It's a grainy photo, captured in sepia tone, showing a large, boarded-up residence, its far left and far right sides cut off by the camera's narrow lens. The home's impressive size and its twin sets of corbels that run along the roof line above the second story suggest its former grandeur. Now, some windows are boarded up and others are missing,

5.3. "Fire Hazard" *(top)*, "Too Close for Comfort" *(bottom)*. Used with permission of Southside Photovoice Project Collection.

making the house appear gap-toothed. Imagine the mental health consequence of the daily confrontation with such obvious neglect. Community psychology literature has focused on the impact of neighborhood quality on the mental health and well-being of its residents: distress, insecurity, and stigma are associated with living in or among substandard housing (Cutrona et al. 2000; Evans 2003; Latkin & Curry 2003).

Another of Faith's poignant photos, "Home That Took Hearts," shown in Figure 5.4, captured the attention of Syracuse University's Chancellor Nancy Cantor. With Faith's permission, she presented the picture in her address at the 2007 Imagining America Conference on the Syracuse University campus (Cantor 2007). The actual image features a beautiful two-story, classically built pink home marred by plywood nailed across the front door and left window. The other windows have been left without plywood, like an unfinished project. In her address, the chancellor remarked,

> This photograph . . . reminds the world of the feeling in this neighborhood where tragedy and loss are signified in the boards that have closed up a beautiful home. Almost a year earlier, a twelve-year-old who loved watching professional wrestling on TV was killed in an accident here when he tried to imitate a wrestling move he had seen on television, the same move that had killed a six-year-old neighbor only two days before. The cameras, the reporters, and the boy's family have all gone away. Only the house remains.

That twelve-year-old was Faith's relative.

Sandra Lane (2008) links the preponderance of dilapidated and abandoned housing in the South Side with increased negative health outcomes like childhood lead poisoning, low birth weight, infant death, and sexually transmitted diseases. She found that the highest rates of lead violations in the city were in areas with high numbers of abandoned housing. In a randomly selected survey of city blocks within census tracts reporting significantly higher poor birth outcomes, she noted:

> We walked and mapped each block, documenting vacant lots, abandoned houses, broken glass, and other types of neighborhood degradation. Among these thirty blocks, there were fourteen abandoned houses and seventy-six vacant or empty lots where houses once stood. Only

5.4. "First Thing I See" *(left)*, "Home That Took Hearts" *(right)*. Used with permission of Southside Photovoice Project Collection.

> four of these thirty blocks had no abandoned houses or vacant lots. In the majority—nineteen of the thirty lots—an average of four houses on each block were either boarded up and abandoned or had been destroyed by fire and demolished, leaving an empty lot on the former site. (Lane, 2008, 41)

To a lesser extent, the women's photos seemed to indict certain local businesses in the persistence of crime and violence within the neighborhood. As was the case with social institutions, the women had already identified many of those businesses through the community mapping exercise. Examples include Gwen's picture of the men's shelter, which she captioned "Unsanitary" to express her disapproval. She also produced images of local convenience storefronts in photos titled "No Place to Be" and "Risky Business."

"No Place to Be" is one of the pictures that Gwen presented at the second Photovoice workshop (Figure 5.5). She captured the image of a boarded-up, defunct convenience store called "A Shack Market." The bottom portion of the building is painted a dull red, and the second story has been left white. The red storefront has gray boards across the windows and doors. There is the ubiquitous "No Loitering" sign that accompanies most boarded buildings in the South Side. The storefront sign, "A Shack Market, full line of grocerie [sic]" is crude, but is remarkably comprehensive in its list of services that extend beyond the sale of ready-to-eat items: "We accept [sic] food stamp, EBT, cash issue." It also accepts payments for cell phones, particularly a line called Cricket, which requires no credit checks, a popular brand among low-income and working-class consumers. In addition to cell phone payments, customers could also make payments to National Grid, the local gas and electric utility.

Gwen's other photo, "Risky Business" (Figure 5.5), shows a busy parking lot at another local convenience store and gas station. Unlike the Shack Market, this store is operational. However, Gwen stressed that the majority of the traffic is outside the store rather than inside. In the upper right-hand corner of the photo, there is yet another "No Loitering" sign. Despite this warning, multiple cars fill the snapshot and mostly male patrons are present. This image reminds me of comments made by Stamps and Stamps (2008) in their characterization of the South Side environment:

> Predominantly Black neighborhoods on the south side revealed an interesting phenomenon. In non-public housing projects, the most visible individuals were men. Most visible around public-housing projects were children and women. During warm weather, children could be seen playing in the street and in the many pocket-size play areas found on the south side. Younger children were supervised by older children rather than by adults. Men hung around bars, cafes, barbershops, service stations, and liquor stores. During the warm weather, they hung out on the street in small and sometimes large groups. In bad weather, they moved inside. The vacant lot next to Phillips Liquor Store was a well-known hangout for men. Year round and regardless of weather, men could be found next to this store. Beer, wine, and hard spirits were purchased and carried to the lot for communal drinking. It was the place where men financially hard up could piece together a bottle. Jokes were told, and "lying on" and "about one's self" was the order of the day. Young men would gravitate to the lot, stand on the periphery, and listen to the tales

5.5. "No Place to Be" (*top*), "Risky Business" (*bottom*). Used with permission of Southside Photovoice Project Collection.

told by older men. Even before the 1980's, Phillips Liquor Store lot and barbershops represented informal schools where young men were social- ized into street corner behavior. (Stamps and Stamps 2008, 202–3)

I interpret their characterization as a gendered arrangement of space, with men occupying public spaces and women occupying less public spaces in and around homes. Stamps and Stamps' perspective on the gathering of local men near convenience stores and lots is more positive than Gwen's interpretation of similar spaces. For Stamps and Stamps, these intergenera- tional gatherings of men served as key sites for socialization and perhaps as a masculine rite of passage for local young men. There is no evidence from the South Side mothers' pictures or dialogue to support the spatial arrangement and socialization described by Stamps and Stamps. In fact, the women view these gatherings of men as a threat to safety, and they try to keep their young sons from "the streets" where the gatherings occur.

Memorials

As noted earlier in the section regarding coding and testing, I uncov- ered a pattern in subjects related to both makeshift and formal memori- als in the South Side mothers' photographs. Nikki and Zora both took photos of roadside memorials created in response to the sudden death of loved ones. Nikki's photo, "Death Knocking," presents a grapevine wreath intertwined with fake flowers attached to the fencepost of a public housing complex. In "Another Life Taken," Zora captures what appears to be glass votives placed around the perimeter of an anemic tree surrounded by con- crete sidewalk. Makeba's documentation of memorial is more literal. She took a photo of the funeral program of a young relative who had recently been murdered. His youthful face is in the center of the program. To the left is the inscription "Sunrise" with the date of his birth in 1988. To the right of his face is the word "Sunset" with the date of his demise in 2007, two months after his nineteenth birthday.

Sometime the women's photographs marked less personal means of memorializing violence and death. As mentioned earlier, two women took photos of the bar where a patron was stabbed. Faith's picture "Home That Took Hearts" does not immediately read as memorial, but its sentiment resounds with grief and worry over a senseless death. Jack Santino refers to these sites of mourning over a sudden death as *spontaneous shrines*: "Central to all of these is the conjunction of the memorializing of personal deaths within the framework of social conditions that caused these deaths, the performative with the commemorative" (2006, 5). In the act of mourning the death of loved one, he distinguishes between a ritualized, private ceremony of a funeral versus a public memorial that highlights a political issue and promotes social change. Street memorials or shrines serve as performative commemoratives, not only calling forth the public to witness but also interpreting the meanings and symbols connected to the site: votive candles, flowers, ribbons, letters, and other personal mementos. He notes that the shrines are "disruptions of the mundane environment," like the two photos from the South Side Photovoice project showing a grapevine wreath on a stretch of fence and a tree surrounded by glass votive holders. He adds, "By translating social issues and political actions into personal terms, the shrines are themselves political statements. Much of their communicative power is derived from their personalization of the public (i.e., performativity) just as a great deal is drawn from the language of mortuary ritual, of death and dying (i.e., of commemoration). They are, I believe, the voice of the people" (2006, 13).

Jonathan Lohman (2006) takes a decidedly less political stance on the meaning behind memorials constructed in an urban setting. His research chronicles the creation and community acceptance of a wall memorial for fifteen youths slain in Philadelphia near 50th Street. He describes the predominantly Black neighborhood in Philly, which has been plagued with drug dealing and street violence, as a "landscape of loss" to the family members and loved one of victims of violence:

> For the families of victims, the landscape around them becomes proliferated with sites of tragedy—pervasive reminders of devastating loss, evoking painful and graphic images . . . one can see how these women feel "stalked" and "haunted" by the landscape around them . . . The experiences of landscape, one's "sense of place," is highly individualized, calling upon a depth of personal experiences and memories. To the families of victims, the experience of landscape will forever be connected with

the tragic losses that these walls have witnessed . . . The [wall on 50th in Philadelphia] memorial, then, could be viewed as a kind of symbolic reclaiming of the wall from death. (2006, 196)

For Lohman, the memorial wall represents a paradox: it becomes a symbol of life for the victim's friends and family and a site of death for everyone else who is not familiar with the victim. Another important element is his discussion of the purely African American cultural form of mourning and funeral practices. The practice of decorating gravesites and other memorials reveals the tendency to blend the worlds of the dead and the living and cements the "renewed connections with the deceased." While he agrees that much of the practice of memorializing has focused on the political, as in the case of Santino (2006), he presents the work around the memorial wall in Philadelphia from the perspective of those families who lost loved ones and what the public site means to them personally.

Natural Environment

Images categorized as natural environment in the analysis of this project include those that captured a landscape, rather than one particular individual or object. This series of photos reflects an affinity for the natural world and incorporates elements of nature, most notably green spaces, water, or both. For example, Katherine presented a park's water feature in her photo entitled "Relaxation." Josephine photographed the spray of water from the fountains at the lake in another local park. The photo's title is "Peace of Mind." However, within the same park she took a negative photo near the water that she called "Waste of Land." Pictured is a close-up of the polluted edge of the lake, clouded by green algae and marked by floating debris. She remarked, "It's so pretty if you're standing far away, but as soon as you get up close—it's trash. It's dirty . . . It just feels like they don't care, it's like people don't care in general . . . it's just beautiful. It's just wasted." Josephine's next photo, entitled "Why," also reflected her frustration with the city in the construction and operation of the Midland Sewage treatment plant in her neighborhood. In the photo a large street sign reads "Road Closed." The foreground shows sparse grass littered with debris, and a construction site looks hazy in the background. In "Why," she illustrated the prolonged interruption of life and traffic on Midland Avenue that the county's newest sewage facility represented to residents of the South Side.

In contrast to spaces of neglect, Harriet provided an image of domestic tranquility within a public housing complex, which she refers to as the "good side." In her photo called "Peace of Mind," the lawns are neatly mowed and are dotted with greenery and decorative pots of flowers. Later, she would tell the audience at the opening of the community exhibition that she did not notice the positive parts of her community until she saw them through the lens of her camera.

Honorable Mentions: Role of Men and Fathering in the South Side

One of the first questions I was asked by the panel of staff members from the local public health agency who helped in the recruitment for the Photovoice project was: what about the men in this neighborhood? It has been my experience that when someone wants to work on issues related to racial minorities, the response is typically "what about everyone else (or whites)?" When I say that I'm working with Black women to define their neighborhood, someone invariably asks me about the men. A Black feminist standpoint suggests that I don't have to consider the other gender; Black women can be the center of analysis and their unique social location implores a focused inquiry on their experiences in a racist and sexist society. So when confronted by that inane question, I grit my teeth and reassert the need to explore Black *women's* experiences. However, people continue to lament, what about the men? One coder even separated out images with men from the Photovoice exercise. So, below I offer a postscript on Black males. Moreover, I demonstrate how the mothers interpret examples of Black fatherhood.

Overall, there were not many adult men featured in the images from the project. Two particular photos are distinct in their juxtaposition of fathers: Nina's "Single Black Father" and Elizabeth's "Untitled (Dad)." Both photos present a Black father, but they diverge in very interesting ways. Elizabeth's photo is in grayscale, and it's grainy. It was clearly taken indoors, perhaps a living room couch. Nina's photo was taken outside; the family is standing on the concrete sidewalk. The dad in Nina's photo is smiling directly into the camera; his body is positioned behind his five children, his arm is draped over the shoulder of one of his sons. Like their father, the children are posed, smiling directly into the camera. Nina chose to highlight her friend, a single Black father, and selected this family photo for the community exhibition: "Those are his kids and finally he has his kids with him . . . He's doing what he's supposed to do, the mother is not around."

Elizabeth's photo shows three boys surrounding their father on a couch. One is sitting on the arm of the couch next to his father, arms crossed and looking directly into the camera. On the other side of the dad, another child leans on his shoulder, eyes closed. The third child is only partially visible; he is sitting on the floor in front of his dad. He faces away from the camera, looking toward his father. The father's attention is not directed at the camera or at any of the boys. He holds a large can of beer in his hand. Elizabeth told the group where his attention is directed: the television. You can tell from the body language of the boys surrounding him that they're seeking his attention, whether by leaning against him or looking at him. However, Elizabeth contends that he is aloof and she is upset by his lack of attention.

Only fifteen of the total 135 photos presented by the South Side mothers during the Photovoice sessions featured adult men, approximately 11 percent. During the first Photovoice session, only ten of the eighty-one images presented featured adult men prominently. There were five pictures with adult men in the fifty-one photos discussed during the second session. I asked each participant to choose two to four pictures that best represent her work for display at the community photography exhibition. When it came time to select images for the exhibition, six photos featuring adult men were chosen among the thirty-seven pictures on display. While I have highlighted contrasting representations of Black fatherhood in the photos, there are also men featured in the photos who serve as mentors. A feminist analysis of the depiction of Black men may focus on the general absence of men and masculine identities rather than on their relative lack of prominence as figures or themes during the Photovoice sessions.

Perhaps one factor in the missing males among these images might be related to the demographics of the South Side community. Lane et al. (2004) point out that there is a 5:4 ratio of Black women to Black men in the city of Syracuse between the ages of twenty and fifty-nine. Moreover, this skewed sex ratio is at its highest between ages twenty and twenty-nine. After ruling out factors linked to birth, death, and migration, the authors conclude that disproportionate incarceration rates among Black men play a large role in their absence in Syracuse, and in women's and children's lives in general. J. S. Jordan-Zachery's article (2008) on the intersection of fatherhood, crime, and urban policies echoes a similar sentiment. Jennifer Hamer (2001) provides an ecological perspective to understand Black fatherhood for noncustodial, low-income black fathers. She differentiates between the microsystem of face-to-face relations that are understood to reflect and reinforce the ideals of fatherhood and to provide support to men in their role as active parents to their children. Examples of this microsystem include the child's mother, extended family, and relatives who help him fulfill his role as father, the employers who allow him time off from work to handle emergencies, and so on. However, the ecological perspective of fatherhood does not end with these intimate relations. These relationships are supported by the macrosystem of relations that include laws, policies, and cultural values that also reinforce and reflect fatherhood ideals. Hamer points out that this macrosystem fails low-income Black men as fathers, in particular because there is a lack of laws and policies in place to address racial disparities in employment and education where this group has fallen short as a social group. Thus, the persistence of unemployment, underemployment, and lack of education coupled with high rates of incarceration make it fundamentally difficult for low-income Black fathers to fulfill the ideal of fatherhood in American society. Hamer criticizes the common discourse of low-income Black fathers as "deadbeat dads," often repeated without a historical, economic, and social context that makes it virtually impossible for them to meet the conditions of socially acceptable fatherhood.

Moreover, legislative initiatives that attempt to address childhood and maternal poverty through marriage promotion efforts persistently neglect to take into account the structural obstacles of Black men. Hence, myths of Black matriarchy prevail, as extolled in Senator Daniel Patrick Moynihan's infamous 1965 report. While Hamer focuses exclusively on the myopia of legislative efforts around marriage promotion as a means to lift the poor out of poverty, Jordan-Zachery indicts a broader set of government initiatives on urban economic development. The assault on the urban poor begins with the Reagan and senior Bush administrations' gutting of welfare programs. In addition, early federal initiatives under the federal highway program, the federal housing program, and increased incarceration of Black men under the federal program's War on Drugs exacerbate racial segregation and spatial isolation of the black poor in inner cities. The interactions of these seemingly disparate policies result in fragility of Black family life. Jerome G. Miller (1996) is much more direct in his articulation of the relationship between the criminal justice system and Black families in his book, *Search and Destroy: African-American Males in the Criminal Justice System.* After providing evidence of the escalating rates of arrests and criminal sentencing of Black men, he concludes that "the criminal justice system itself has been a major contributor to breakdown in the inner cities." While I don't have the evidence to explain the relative absence of Black men in the South Side mothers' images, it is useful to consider the broader context of factors that lead to missing Black men.

The Community Exhibition

I have cried in the line of duty at least three times. The most recent was during the course of this project. The first time was during People's Earth Day 1995 in the Bayview Hunters Point community of San Francisco. I had previously watched my senior colleague at Greenpeace, Bradley Angel, puff up his slight frame and appear nearly six feet tall when he confronted shady corporate characters and ineffective bureaucrats in his staunch support of community activists fighting for environmental justice. That day in April 1995, I decided to borrow a page from Bradley's playbook: prior to the start of the fair, I approached the booth of the San Francisco Energy Company. I was working with a community group in Bayview Hunters Point, the Southeast Alliance for Environmental Justice (SAEJ), fighting the construction of a third power plant in their neighborhood as proposed by San Francisco Energy (SFE), a subsidiary of AES Energy Corporation. Ironically, SFE representatives decided to advertise the benefits of their plants at an Earth Day celebration. Horror of horrors! Well, I was not going to stand for it. With a mythical Bradley perched upon my shoulder, I marched up to the fair organizers and demanded that SFE leave the fair. For me, their presence was in direct opposition to the goals of the fair and to Earth Day in general. Here, an active group within the community had launched a campaign against this company, yet they were invited to tout the environmental benefits of a gas-burning power plant in an already overburdened neighborhood. Little did I know that SFE had secured a very powerful community ally who blasted me, publicly. I was shocked and stunned and don't even remember walking away with tears in my eyes. I was no Bradley Angel.

The second cry in the line of duty took place during the final years of my doctoral program at the University of Michigan. After my four-year stint at Greenpeace, I considered graduate school relatively conflict-free—until the day I gathered my doctoral committee members together to discuss my plans to finish the program. I had an ambitious plan to complete my doctoral program. I wanted to take my preliminary examination within the next semester and to promptly move to a dissertation proposal defense a few short months later. However, when I reviewed my plans during the committee meeting, one of the professors voiced strong opposition to my accelerated pace. I was flummoxed. There was no big secret to my plan. I had talked to each of the members individually. This meeting was supposed to be merely a formality. I had not anticipated opposition. This member's stance was inflexible, and there was a tense silence as we all tried to figure out how to proceed around an immovable object of "hell, no." I closed the meeting awkwardly and promptly started my pity fest in a stall of the bathroom of the Dana building on the Ann Arbor campus. I cried in the line of duty, as I had in San Francisco years before.

The most recent cry in the line of duty occurred during the course of this community mapping and Photovoice project. The community-based partner was the local health clinic on the South Side. Over the course of the project, our working relationship deteriorated. There seemed to be a degree of mistrust. Changes that I initiated over the course of the project were perceived as intentional deceptions. In retrospect, I should have spent as much time and reflection on gaining the trust of the project's cosponsors as I did with the participants. I made unrealistic assumptions that the representatives from the local health center were in agreement with the social change component of the project. I was wrong.

A few days before the community exhibition's grand opening, I was summoned to an emergency meeting. They were concerned about the social justice frame in the advertising of the exhibition. They demanded to see and have final approval of the images being presented. No pictures were removed from the exhibition. Instead, they requested the removal of the name of the health center from all promotional advertising. The entire exchange blindsided me, and I found myself in tears, once again, in the parking lot.

Despite the last-minute drama, the exhibition opened with a program on the afternoon of Saturday, July 28, 2007, at the Community Folk Art Center, an extension of the African American Studies Department at Syracuse University. Shirley, Harriet, CJ, Makeba, and Josephine brought their families to admire their photography. The group selected Billie to formally address the gathering. However, all the women spoke about the project in the end. The exhibition ran throughout the summer. The following fall, the exhibition moved to the Syracuse campus. There were plans to exhibit at the local health center, but relations had become so strained that it didn't happen immediately. Before long, I was on bed rest and had to put many of my plans on hold.

Recall that this project was designed to explore poor Black mothers' notions of the environment. Initially I presumed that there would be numerous images related to the construction of the wastewater treatment site, along with visible signs of urban decay. However, the mothers' images revealed much more. In fact, most of the photos chosen were positive images filled with friends, family, and recreation.

What do we make of all of these images? What can we surmise about the South Side mothers in relation to the lives and experiences of Black women in underserved communities everywhere? These photographs offer an authentic glimpse into the lived experiences of these moms. Their images are full of the positive influences of their children, mentor and kin networks, stable social institutions, and the natural environment. All these mitigate the impact of their images that represent the death, drugs, and violence that plague their community. This work illuminates the struggles of South Side women. In the midst of what we may see as gritty experience and hard times, they have a great degree of pride about their homes and families. Most revealing is not necessarily the links between South Side mothers and other inner city mothers, but between them and women around the globe who are forced to provide protection for themselves and their families in chaotic spaces. From Belfast to the South Side, Photovoice balances the relationship between researcher and subject, creating an authentic voice of mothers and upholding the epistemologies of Black feminism that calls attention to the intersection of race, class, and gender. It is my wish that this project restore dignity and visibility to Black women, who are often ignored or misunderstood.

6

Conclusion

Evaluating Spatial Strategies in
Feminist Theorizing and Research

My goal for this book was to build a bridge between Black feminist theory and environmental justice scholarship by expounding on the lived experiences of Black women in an impoverished urban neighborhood. To this end, my task was not only to point out the structural obstacles that make living, working, and playing in a space of environmental neglect particularly challenging but also to highlight the strength and agency of those low-income, African American mothers who are able to prosper in the face of such obstacles. In other words, I set out to investigate both structure and agency. In the preceding chapters, I have presented arguments for the integration of spatial theorizing in Black feminist epistemology and the usefulness of spatial and visual research methodologies to explore how Black mothers raise their families within an environmentally degraded community. This chapter evaluates the strength of the relations between space, race, gender, agency, and environmental justice. Overall, I think that this integration of elements contributes to feminist applications such as intersectionality and the matrix of domination. I contend that these ideas are also inherently spatial; they are spatial in their ontological construction of oppressions and their multiplicative effects. Moreover, resistance to forms of patriarchy, racism, and class domination has often taken the form of both physical and intellectual resistance through the occupation of these oppressive spaces.

Space and Race

In chapter 3, I applied the racialized space hypothesis to describe the cycles of disruption and dislocation of African Americans in Syracuse since the 1930s. Those who have studied urban history have found that the sixties period of urban renewal formed the cornerstone of Black community upheaval. Through archival research, I have uncovered the persistent patterns of demolition and reconstruction, particularly among predominantly Black areas in the city of Syracuse, as early as the 1935 demolition of the poor area referred to as Washington-Water Strip. Discriminatory practices in housing by white homeowners, later codified by federal government programs like the Home Owners' Loan Corporation, made Black spaces vulnerable to the whims of the city's growth machine. Each step that the growth machine and city planners hailed as progress (a new highway, public housing projects, a bus transfer station, a museum, a county sewage treatment plant, etc.) inevitably led to the sacrifice of Black spaces and to forced resettlement. Although Syracuse is presented here as a case study, its African Americans are not alone in their struggle against the growth machine; this happens to Black communities in major cities across the United States. The strength of the racialized space hypothesis may also be its greatest weakness. It is preoccupied with larger external forces that create racial landscapes and deems those within certain areas as inferior. Where space is an exercise in power for the dominant interests in society, the contestation of that power by marginalized people is rooted in protest through space.

For social movements, reclaiming and renaming space is a source of pride among activists and constitutes a way to measure success in the campaign for justice. There are numerous examples. During the civil rights struggle, contestation of space was manifested in lunch counter sit-ins at establishments that refused to serve Black patrons. These sit-ins constituted a form of space claiming: protestors were proclaiming, *We are here and we will be acknowledged.* Nearly half a century before the modern civil rights era, Homer Plessy entered white space on a New Orleans streetcar and refused to leave. He occupied space that had been prohibited to him and reclaimed it as his own in the fight for integration. Another common strategy has been the lock-in on college campuses. The idea behind a lock-in is that students reclaim the space of college administrators to remind them of whose interests they should ultimately serve. An environmental activist strategy is the lockdown, where activists physically chain themselves to trees, fenceposts, or other objects to bear witness to environmental harm. Whether it is a sit-in, lock-in, or lockdown, these strategies by social justice groups recognize space as a form of power and assert their power by reclaiming those spaces.

What are the implications of the idea that space is power? Racialized space speaks to a process that includes both spatial and temporal dimensions and affirms the idea that the disproportionate impacts borne by communities of color and the poor today result from historical acts. I believe that it is important to highlight the chronology of Black spaces within the city of Syracuse in order to understand the social problems that plague the South Side community today. Understanding that space is power shows that urban planning, both past and present, is critical to the growth and sustainability of communities of color. Thus, if space was an organizing tool for oppression in the past, it is fair to assume that a spatial reorganization must take place to insure equality in the future.

The racialized space argument has a tendency to create villains and victims. Thus, it would be unfair to characterize these forms of spatial oppression without highlighting the ways in which Blacks and other racial and ethnic minorities have exercised agency through collective resistance to those spaces. In fact, a discussion of urban renewal projects in Syracuse must acknowledge the strong role and effective organizing of the Congress of Racial Equality (CORE), the local NAACP, and the Urban League. Today, groups like the Partnership for Onondaga Creek, Syracuse United Neighbors, and others continue to fight for equal rights and fair treatment. At the heart of these struggles is the fight for recognition and visibility. Just as in the case of Forest Grove and Center Springs in Louisiana, the impact of the growth machine's projects on Syracuse's Black residents has been denied outright or underestimated. Many agree that the struggle for civil rights has been a campaign for humanity and collective resistance against oppressive spaces. James Tyner's work (2006, 2007) focuses on the spatial project inherent in the Black power movement and its leaders, Malcolm X, Stokely Carmichael, H. Rap Brown, Huey Newton, and Eldridge Cleaver, among others. Black radicals sought to reorganize spaces, particularly urban spaces. Tyner takes time to differentiate between the struggle for civil rights in the South based on integrationist strategies and the urban campaigns for racial justice in the Northern and Western United States, which focused instead on achieving control of their communities, rather than seeking inclusion in white spaces.

Against the backdrop of racist housing and urban renewal policies, Tyner points out that the rhetoric of Black radicals in the 1960s served as critiques of socio-spatial relations. Rather than adopting an integration-based rationale like the Southern campaigns, Black radicals sought what he terms *communal separatism*. He defines this phrase as "separate communities, such as Black towns, wherein African Americans retain political, economic, and social control of their surroundings. Integration, for these black radical intellectuals, was a capitulation to domination. Integration policies, according to these intellectuals, deprived African Americans of their fundamental right to self-determination. To integrate in a white supremacist society was to negate the spaces of African Americans" (2007, 226–30). In his book, *The Geography of Malcolm X*, Tyner acknowledges that the catalyst for X's later political transformation from a leader in the Nation of Islam to a Pan Africanist was displacement: both a ideological displacement from the Nation of Islam and a physical displacement from the United States toward the end of his life. Displacement is a process I describe in the Black community experience in Syracuse. More specifically, critical geography provides evidence of seventy years of displacement for African American families by the city's growth machine. Three cycles of disruption and displacement form the prism through which we can view the contemporary experiences of the South Side mothers within this study.

While social movements for Black power, civil rights, and the environmental justice are critical in this rupture of oppressive spaces and the continuing struggle for liberation, I've chosen to focus on the lived experiences of a small group of mothers in Syracuse South Side. I wanted to know how they made sense of their community. I understood that their agency was not necessarily exercised through direct challenges to the oppressive spaces within the South Side but rather through creating a network of supportive individuals and stable institutions that assist in their place making. Despite the threat of violence and personal and financial hardships, these women are proud of their homes, their families, and themselves. This strength and fortitude is the manifestation of their agency and resistance to an oppressive space.

Katherine McKittrick and Clyde Woods have advocated the practice of black geographies: "Insert[ing] black geographies into our worldview and our understanding of spatial liberation and other emancipatory strategies can perhaps move us away from territoriality, the normative practice of staking claim to place . . . those who 'no one knows' might also be a map towards a new or different perspective on the production of space" (2007, 5). The mothers from the South Side who participated in this project are "those who 'no one knows.'" Understanding how they make sense of their environment and find meaning and support in their community offers an alternative perspective, as McKittrick and Woods have suggested. Through their images, maps, and narratives, the South Side's gritty urban landscape of streets and structures evolve into a network of neighbors, community, and spiritual centers that combat the negative influences of violence, gangs, drug use, and trafficking.

Black Women and Space

In chapters 4 and 5 I proposed that the best way to address the link between gender and space is via two research methodologies: community mapping and Photovoice. Community mapping offers a means for defining the South Side community from within, as well as a lens to explore the relative safety and security of specific areas in the South Side according to the project participants. However, community mapping may have its limitations. If I contend that spatial organization is an important construct to measure and test spatiality, creating a predefined map has already imposed explicit boundaries. On the other hand, asking participants to draw a map by hand may be an exercise in testing their spatial literacy rather than exploring their spatiality. There are trade-offs in the community mapping exercise I used. My decision to opt for uniformity and conduct the exercise as a form of consensus may have limited the participants' imaginations. In fact some participants marked their maps with labels for areas beyond the drawn boundaries. Future community mapping exercises may want to explore both approaches.

Photovoice built on the mapping exercise by expanding the sites identified as safe and unsafe with visual images and narratives from the South Side mothers. By comparing the pattern of images that emerged with those of other Photovoice projects, common themes about the importance of family and sisterhood emerged. The originator of the Photovoice method, Caroline Wang, has always based this methodology on feminist principles; she asserts that this technique gives voice to women. I've attempted to extend the tenets of feminism in general and Black feminism in particular to Photovoice. Black feminist ideologies are inherently spatial. Black feminists have often identified the multiple ways in which poor Black women in particular are oppressed, through not only racism but also sexism and classism, and they reject attempts to place a hierarchy on these forms of oppression. To avoid hierarchical jargon, these theorists use terms to describe multiple oppressions as *interlocking* or *intersectional*: the terms lend themselves to a socio-spatial imagining of oppressions that is nonlinear and nonvertical.

The gender-space framework that I imagine includes interlocking spheres of oppression due to racism, sexism, classism, homophobia, and ability. Related to my arguments on space and race, it would be remiss to describe gender oppression without giving voice to agency. Like those who argue for racial equality, those who strive for gender equality have sought greater understanding for the humanity of women, recognition of women, and gendered ways of knowing, and have called for a reorganization of space that includes and embraces women. The gender project has advocated for the reassertion of women and their experiences into history and social life. Again, we see the project as a rupture of patriarchal spaces in order to include women. Among Black feminists, this rupture has manifested itself with the pen, rather than through physical demonstrations against oppressive spaces like the sit-ins at lunch counters of the early civil rights movement. Writers like Audre Lorde, bell hooks, Angela Davis, Kimberly Crenshaw, and others have sought to teach us the ways in which Black women's experiences have been erased or rendered invisible. In her book *Demonic Grounds*, McKittrick (2006) analyzes Black women's geographies throughout the African Diaspora in confrontation with the geography of domination. Here, geography of domination is evidenced through the horrors of transatlantic slavery and the subsequent racial-sexual displacement of Black women's bodies. She posits that Black matters are spatial matters, and that Black feminism and humanness are inextricably bound within this geographic struggle from spatial domination. She expounds on this in her examination of texts that include Harriet Jacobs' *Incidents in the Life of a Slave Girl*, Robbie McCauley's *Sally's Rape*, Octavia Butler's *Kindred*, and Toni Morrison's *Sites of Memory*. These texts illustrate the geography of domination and erasure while simultaneously revealing Black women's individual control and agency in the recapture of their spaces and the extension of memories.

It is thanks to their writings and influence that I am able to write my own narrative of experiencing space in relation to my own race, gender, and class location. During the project, I came up against the issue of the insider/outsider position: On the one hand, I saw myself as one of the women in the project. I too grew up poor and working class with a single mother. I also faced the kind of personal and financial hardships that the South Side mothers had to deal with and I knew the threat of violence from drugs and gangs in my community. On the other hand, as a professor from an elite local university, I also had cachet in a world of privilege. In their eyes, I lived worlds apart from their experience. After all, I didn't know the location of the local clothing discount store in Shop City! Thus, I found myself in this strange limbo—stuck between my humble upbringing and the privileged world, one that my own grandmother could not imagine. Inhabiting this privileged world, I've often found myself at odds with those around me and uncomfortable in a place where access to resources is taken for granted and entitlements are unearned. This creates a tension within me. I feel like a fraud. I've accumulated too much wealth and knowledge to ever go back to my understanding of the world before I left home at the age of eighteen.

I have to tamp down my initial reactions to situations that occur in my new middle-class lifestyle. I have vestiges of the same vigilance that the women discuss in the community mapping chapter, the frozen watchfulness for potential threats around me. I was sure that this vigilance would fade as

I became upwardly mobile. However, this sensitivity has been enhanced by my choice of profession. Becoming an academic means assuming a level of expertise, which remains open to challenge and debate. This role has actually reignited my vigilance in many ways, as I test to see if each perceived slight is due to racist or sexist motives.

This idea of hypervigilance is raised in Diane Brown et al. (2003). There is a stress-related threat of racial discrimination experienced by some African Americans; a heightened guardedness that may be the result of coping with historical roots of racial discrimination. Renee White chronicled her own insider/outsider status as a Black female researcher in her ethnographic work on the factors that lead to the higher rates of HIV among young Black and Latina women. She writes, "Many saw my status as a reflection of an elite lifestyle . . . If people saw me as actively participating in a social reality that fundamentally rejected them, by extension this meant that my own racial-ethnic gender identity had to be compromised" (White 2008, 286). Patricia Hill Collins's work involved the plight of Black female academics in her description of the politics of containment, yet another spatially derived term to describe gender and racial oppression, this time in the academy. She writes that one of the critical elements in the new politics of containment is surveillance: "Where segregation used to keep Black women out of the classroom and boardroom, surveillance now becomes an important mechanism of control" (Collins 1998, 39). She begins by emphasizing the connection between knowledge production and power and its implication for Black women intellectuals.

While I suspect that my honest narrative of my life as contextualized with experiences of the South Side mothers may be applauded by some, many may criticize my reliance on mapping to start the discussion about gender and racial justice in this project. After all, mapping has been and continues to be used as a rationalization for the partitioning of space and the legitimacy of knowledge and power. Mapping Blackness has been described as limiting and deterministic (McKittrick 2006). With this criticism in mind, I strived for balance between highlighting structure inherent in planning maps and accounting for agency in presenting the South Side mothers' maps. Using critical geography, I sought to interrogate the assumptions made in the urban planning and redevelopment maps of

Syracuse. I wholeheartedly acknowledge the determinism in those maps, and I engaged in a process of understanding the racial assumptions and beliefs that the maps conveyed, coupled with the real consequences of disruption and dislocation for Black lives within those spaces.

Mine is the first book-length project involving Photovoice. Interdisciplinary in tone and content, it borrows ideas from the fields of geography, sociology, history, community psychology, and public health. As a consequence, this text may invite criticism when examined from a singular academic field.

Years have passed between the conclusion of my workshops with the South Side mothers and the completion of this book. In the intervening time in Syracuse, certain political ironies emerged. First, former Congressman James T. ("Jim") Walsh—the son of the mayor who ushered in the city's urban renewal projects—was responsible in securing millions of dollars in funds for the same area under the federal enterprise zone program (Sieh 2003). This program targets underdeveloped areas within major cities for the purpose of business revitalization and economic development. Jim Walsh campaigned to revitalize the neighborhood that his father William F. Walsh tore down in the name of progress over forty years earlier. The second irony is that a Syracuse Common Councilperson has proposed the removal of the elevated portion of Interstate 81; the same interstate that cut off portions of Pioneer Homes public housing and demolished living space that spurred South Side neighborhood decline in the sixties. The final irony is that after the Midland Sewage treatment plant was built and the enormous pipeline that tore up the southern and western sections of the city was installed, the Onondaga County Executive approved plans to scrap the construction of an additional site in downtown Syracuse, opting for the use of environmentally friendly technology to further remediate the county's sewage problems. Past projects from the Syracuse growth machine that displaced thousands of African Americans are today seen as boondoggles.

The time between the conclusion of the workshops and the completion of this book also represented personal milestones. I had to recover from my pregnancy loss. I had to understand the impact of my own racial, ethnic, and class identities as part of the construction, operation, and analysis of the research. I had to find my voice and bring forth my narrative in a way that would provide a richer context to the project and the voices of the South Side mothers. I walked into this project in 2007, not understanding the depth to which it would take me on my own personal journey as a Black woman. I'm proud and amazed that I was part of carving out a space that turbulent summer—a space that was not only safe in the midst of uncertainty and chaos but one that also became a source of sisterhood and comfort. I regret that it could not have lasted longer and that my plans to move the group toward social change and action remained unfulfilled. Time and distance has made it easier for me to grasp and to accept the fact that while the South Side project could not be continued, it has left indelible effects upon all those who were part of it.

Nana would be so proud.

REFERENCES

INDEX

References

Aalbers, Manuel B. 2006. "'When the Banks Withdraw, Slum Landlords Take Over': The Structuration of Neighbourhood Decline through Redlining, Drug Dealing, Speculation, and Immigrant Exploitation." *Urban Studies* 43, no. 7: 1061–86.

Andrews, Ralph, and Alan K. Campbell. 1964. *The Negro in Syracuse: His Education, Employment, Income and Housing.* Syracuse: Univ. College of Syracuse Univ.

Baker, Tamara A., and Caroline Wang. 2006. "Photovoice: Use of a Participatory Action Research Method to Explore the Chronic Pain Experience in Older Adults." *Qualitative Health Research* 16, no. 10: 1405–13.

Bevc, Christine, Brent Marshall, and J. Picou. 2007. "Environmental Justice and Toxic Exposure: Toward a Spatial Model of Physical Well-being." *Social Science Research* 36: 48–67.

Booth, Tim, and Wendy Booth. 2003. "In the Frame: Photovoice and Mothers with Learning Difficulties." *Disability & Society* 18, no. 4: 431–42.

Brazg, Tracy, Betty Bekemeier, Clarence Spigner, and Colleen E. Huebner. 2011. "Our Community in Focus: The Use of Photovoice for Youth-Driven Substance Abuse Assessment and Health Promotion." *Health Promotion Practice* 12, no. 4: 502–11.

Brodsky, Anne E. 2000. "The Role of Religion in the Lives of Resilient, Urban, African American, Single Mothers." *Journal of Community Psychology* 28, no. 2: 199–219.

Brown, Diane R. 2003. "A Conceptual Model of Mental Health Well-being for African American Women." In *In and Out of Our Right Minds: The Mental Health of African American Women*, edited by D. R. Brown and V. M. Keith, 1–19. New York: Columbia Univ. Press.

Brown, Diane R., Verna M. Keith, James S. Jackson, and Lawrence E. Gary. 2003. "(Dis)Respected and (Dis)Regarded: Experiences of Racism and Psychological

Distress." In *In and Out of Our Right Minds: The Mental Health of African American Women*, edited by D. R. Brown and V. M. Keith, 83–99. New York: Columbia Univ. Press.

Brown, Phil, and Faith Ferguson. 1995. "'Making a Big Stink': Women's Work, Women's Relationships and Toxic Waste Victims." *Gender and Society* 9, no. 2: 145–72.

Bruce, Marino A., and Michael C. Thornton. 2004. "It's My World? Exploring Black and White Perceptions of Personal Control." *The Sociological Quarterly* 45, no. 3: 597–612.

Bukowski, Kate, and Stephen Buetow. 2011. "Making the Invisible Visible: A Photovoice Exploration of Homeless Women's Health and Lives in Central Auckland." *Social Science & Medicine* 72, no. 5: 739.

Bullard, Robert D. 1998. *Confronting Environmental Racism: The Case of Shintech and Convent, Louisiana Department of Environmental Quality Hearing.* January 24, 1998.

Cantor, Nancy. 2007. "Welcome Address: Imagining America; Imagining Universities: Who and What?" Paper read at Imagining America Annual Conference, September 7, 2007, at Syracuse Univ., Syracuse, NY.

Carlson, Elizabeth D., Joan Engebretson, and Robert M. Chamberlain. 2006. "Photovoice as a Social Process of Critical Consciousness." *Qualitative Health Research* 16, no. 6: 836–52.

Clark, Cammie. 2005. "Displaced Families Struggle to Create New Homes." *The Post-Standard*, March 17, 2005, B1.

Clinton, William J. 1994. Executive Order 12898: Federal Actions to Address Environmental Justice in Minority Populations and Low-income Populations.

Collins, Patricia Hill. 1990. *Black Feminist Thought: Knowledge, Consciousness and the Politics of Empowerment.* London: Harper Collins Academic.

———. 1998. *Fighting Words: Black Women and the Search for Justice*, vol. 7 of *Contradictions of Modernity.* Minneapolis: Univ. of Minnesota Press.

———. 1999. "Shifting the Center: Race, Class and Feminist Theorizing about Motherhood." In *American Families: A Multicultural Reader*, edited by S. Coontz, M. Parson, and G. Raley, 197–217. New York: Routledge.

Cornwall, Andrea, Fernanda Capibaribe, and Terezinha Gonçalves. 2010. "Revealed Cities: A Photovoice Project with Domestic Workers in Salvador, Brazil." *Development* 53, no. 2: 299–300.

Crampton, Jeremy W. 2010. *Mapping: A Critical Introduction to Cartography and GIS.* West Sussex, UK: Wiley-Blackwell.

Cutrona, C. E., D. W. Russel, and V. Murry. 2000. "Direct and Moderating Effects of Community Context on the Psychological Well-being of African American Women." *Journal of Personality and Social Psychology* 79, no. 6: 1088–101.

Darby, Golden B. 1937. *The Negro in Syracuse: A Study in Community Relations.* Syracuse: Dunbar Center.

Davies, Carole Boyce. 2007. *Left of Karl Marx: The Political Life of Black Communist Claudia Jones.* Durham, NC: Duke Univ. Press.

Davis, Barbara Sheklin. 1980. "A History of the Black Community of Syracuse: Exhibition & Symposium." Syracuse: Onondaga Community College.

Davis, Mike. 1992. *City of Quartz : Excavating the Future in Los Angeles.* New York: Vintage Books.

Department of Geography. 1963. *Family Relocations from Syracuse Urban Renewal Area.* Syracuse: Syracuse Univ.

DiChiro, Giovana. 1998. "Environmental Justice from the Grassroots." In *The Struggles for Ecological Democracy: Environmental Justice Movements in the United States*, edited by D. Faber, 104–36. New York: Guilford Press.

Dill, Bonnie Thornton, and Ruth Enid Zambrana. 2009. "Critical Thinking about Inequality: An Emerging Lens." In *Emerging Intersections: Race, Class, and Gender in Theory, Policy, and Practice*, edited by B. T. Dill and R. E. Zambrana, 1–21. New Brunswick, NJ: Rutgers Univ. Press.

Douglas, Amber N., Sherlyn Jimenez, Hsiu-Ju Lin, and Linda K. Frisman. 2008. "Ethnic Differences in the Effects of Spiritual Well-being on Long-term Psychological and Behavioral Outcomes within a Sample of Homeless Women." *Cultural Diversity and Ethnic Minority Psychology* 14, no. 4: 344–52.

Dowty, Douglass. 2007. "How New Police Unit Maps Syracuse Crime: Criminal Intelligence Unit Aims to Prevent Crimes with Data." *The Post-Standard*, July 30, 2007, B1.

Ducre, Kishi Animashaun. 2006. "Racialized Spaces and the Emergence of Environmental Injustice." In *Echoes from the Poisoned Well: Global Memories of Environmental Injustice*, edited by S. H. Washington, P. Rosier, and H. Goodall, 109–24. Lanham, MD: Rowman & Littlefield.

———. 2007. "Katrina as Postscript to Racialized Spaces in Louisiana." In *Seeking Higher Ground: The Race, Public Policy and Hurricane Katrina Crisis Reader*, edited by M. Marable, I. Steinberg, and K. Clarke-Avery, 65–74. New York: Palgrave MacMillan.

Evans, G. W. 2003. "The Built Environment and Mental Health." *Journal of Urban Health* 80, no. 4: 536–55.

Evans, G. W., and E. Kantrowitz. 2002. "Socioeconomic Status and Health: The Potential Role of Environmental Risk Exposure." *Annual Review of Public Health* 23: 303–31.

Fainstein, Susan. 1997. "Justice, Politics, and the Creation of Urban Space." In *The Urbanization of Justice*, edited by E. Swyngedouw, 18–44. New York: New York Univ. Press.

Federal Home Loan Bank Board (FHLBB). 1937. *Security Area Descriptions for Syracuse, New York*. Record Group 195 [records of the Federal Home Loan Bank Board, Home Owners' Loan Corporation, 1933–21, and records related to the City Survey File, 1935–40]. National Archives II, College Park, MD.

Fish, M. 2006a. "Crisis Shuts Youth Center: Syracuse Housing Authority, Facing $1 Million Deficit Shuts Central Village." *The Post-Standard*, July 1, 2006, B1.

———. 2006b. "Boys & Girls Club Seek Reopening Aid; Groups Wants United Way to Reopen Shonnard, Central Village Sites." *The Post-Standard*, December 8, 2006, B2.

Foster-Fishman, Pennie, Branda Nowell, Zermarie Deacon, M. Angela Nievar, and Peggy McCann. 2005. "Using Methods That Matter: The Impact of Reflection, Dialogue, and Voice." *American Journal of Community Psychology* 36 nos. 3–4: 275–91.

Freire, Paulo. 2002. *Pedagogy of the Oppressed*. 30th Anniversary Edition. New York: Continuum.

Fullilove, Mindy Thompson. 2004. *Root Shock: How Tearing up City Neighborhoods Hurts America, and What We Can Do about It*. New York: One World/Ballantine Books.

Gilbert, M. R. 1998. "'Race,' Space, and Power: The Survival Strategies of Working Poor Women." *Annals of the Association of American Geographers* 88, no. 4: 595–621.

Goodhart, Fern Walter, Joanne Hsu, Ji H. Baek, Adrienne L. Coleman, Francesca M. Maresca, and Marilyn B. Miller. 2006. "A View through a Different Lens: Photovoice as a Tool for Student Advocacy." *Journal of American College Health* 55: 53–56.

Greene, Orville H. 1938. Letter from Acting Chairman of the Syracuse Housing Authority. Syracuse, May 18, 1938.

Hamer, Jennifer. 2001. *What It Means to Be Daddy: Fatherhood for Black Men Living away from Their Children*. New York: Columbia Univ. Press.

Harris, Rosalind. 2005. "The Impact of Violence, Crime, and Gangs in the African American Community." In *Contemporary Mental Health Issues Among African Americans*, edited by D. A. Harley and J. M. Dillard, 175–90. Alexandria, VA: American Counseling Association.

Harvey, David. 1973. *Social Justice and the City*. London: Edward Arnold.

———. 1996. *Justice, Nature and the Geography of Difference*. Cambridge, MA: Blackwell Publishers.

Hawkins, B. D. 1988. "Oxford Inn Offers Shelter, Makes Few Demands." *The Post-Standard*, B3.

Hergenrather, Kenneth C., Scott D. Rhodes, and Glenn Clark. 2006. "Windows to Work: Exploring Employment-Seeking Behaviors of Persons with HIV/AIDS through Photovoice." *AIDS Education and Prevention* 18, no. 3: 243–58.

Hillier, Amy E. 2003. "Spatial Analysis of Historical Redlining: A Methodological Exploration." *Journal of Housing Research* 14, no. 1: 137–67.

———. 2005. "Residential Security Maps and Neighborhood Appraisals: The Home Owners' Loan Corporation and the Case of Philadelphia." *Social Science History* 29, no. 2: 207–33.

hooks, bell. 1995. "Black Women: Shaping Feminist Theory." In *Words of Fire: An Anthology of African-American Feminist Thought*, edited by B. Guy-Sheftall, 270–82. New York: The New Press.

International Visual Methodologies for Social Change Project (IVM). 2006. *Doing Photo-Voice*. Available from http: //www.ivmproject.ca/photo_voice.php.

———. n.d. "On the Uses of Photo-voice by Teacher and Community Health Care Workers Working with Youth in Rural KwaZulu-Natal to Address HIV & AIDS." Montreal, QC: McGill Univ.

Jackson, Kenneth. 1985. *Crabgrass Frontier: The Suburbanization of the United States*. Oxford, UK: Oxford Univ. Press.

Jones, Nikki. 2010. *Between Good and Ghetto: African American Girls and Inner-City Violence*. The Rutgers Series in Childhood Studies. New Brunswick, NJ: Rutgers Univ. Press.

Jones, Robert Emmet, and Shirley A. Rainey. 2006. "Examining Linkages between Race Environmental Concern, Health, and Justice in a Highly Polluted Community of Color." *Journal of Black Studies* 36, no. 4: 473–96.

Jordan-Zachery, J. S. 2008. "Policy Interaction: The Mixing of Fatherhood, Crime and Urban Policies." *Journal of Social Policy* 37, no. 1: 81–102.

Killion, Cheryl M., and Caroline C. Wang. 2000. "Linking African American Mothers across Life Stage and Station through Photovoice." *Journal of Health Care for the Poor and Underserved* 11, no. 3: 310–25.

King, Deborah. 1988. "Multiple Jeopardy, Multiple Consciousness: The Context of a Black Feminist Ideology." *Signs: Journal of Women in Culture and Society* 14, no. 1: 42–72.

Klawiter, M. 1999. "Racing for the Cure, Walking Women, and Toxic Touring: Mapping Cultures of Action within the Bay Area Terrain of Breast Cancer." *Social Problems* 46, no. 1: 104–26.

Lane, Sandra D. 2008. *Why Are Our Babies Dying? Pregnancy, Birth, and Death in America*. Boulder: Paradigm Publishers.

Lane, Sandra D., R. H. Keefe, R. A. Rubinstein, B. A. Levandowski, M. Freedman, A. Rosenthal, D. A. Cibula, and M. Czerwinski. 2004. "Marriage Promotion and Missing Men: African American Women in a Demographic Double Bind." *Medical Anthropology Quarterly* 18, no. 4: 405–28.

Latkin, C. A., and A. D. Curry. 2003. "Stressful Neighborhoods and Depression: A Prospective Study on the Impact of Neighborhood Disorder." *Journal of Health and Social Behavior* 44, no. 1: 34–44.

Lawson, Bill. 2001. "Living for the City: Urban United States and Environmental Justice." In *Faces of Environmental Racism*, edited by L. Westra and B. E. Lawson, 41–56. Lanham, MD: Rowman & Littlefield.

Leavy, P. 2009. "The Visual Arts." In *Method Meets Art*, 215–38. New York: Guilford Press.

Linton, Rhoda. 1990. "Toward a Feminist Research Method." In *Gender/Body/Knowledge*, edited by A. Jaggar and S. Bordo, 273–92. New Brunswick, NJ: Rutgers Univ. Press.

Liu, Feng. 2001. *Environmental Justice Analysis: Theories, Methods, and Practice*. Boca Raton, FL: Lewis Publishers.

Lohman, Jonathan. 2006. "A Memorial Wall in Philadelphia." In *Spontaneous Shrines and Public Memorializations of Death*, edited by J. Santino, 177–214. New York: Palgrave Macmillan.

Lopez, Ellen D. S., Eugenia Eng, Naomi Robinson, and C. Wang. 2005. "Photovoice as a Community-Based Participatory Research Method: A Case Study with African American Breast Cancer Survivors in Rural Eastern North Carolina." In *Methods in Community-Based Participatory Research for Health*, edited by B. A. Israel, E. Eng, A. J. Schulz, and E. A. Parker, 326–48. San Francisco: Jossey-Bass.

Lorde, Audre. 1995. "Age, Race, Class, and Sex: Women Redefining Difference." In *Words of Fire: An Anthology of African-American Feminist Thought*, edited by B. Guy-Sheftall, 284–91. New York: The New Press.

Lyttle-Pierce, Alicia. Forthcoming. "Louisiana Photovoice." Ph.D. diss., School of Natural Resources and the Environment, Univ. of Michigan, Ann Arbor.

Maantay, J. 2002. "Mapping Environmental Injustices: Pitfalls and Potential of Geographic Information Systems in Assessing Environmental Health and Equity." *Environmental Health Perspectives* 110: 161–71.

Mahmood, Atiya, Habib Chaudhury, Yvonne L. Michael, Michael Campo, Kara Hay, and Ann Sarte. 2012. "A Photovoice Documentation of the Role of Neighborhood Physical and Social Environments in Older Adults' Physical Activity in Two Metropolitan Areas in North America." *Social Science & Medicine* 74, no. 8: 1180.

Marable, Manning, and Leith Mullings. 2003. *Let Nobody Turn Us Around: Voices of Resistance, Reform, and Renewal*. Lanham, MD: Rowman & Littlefield.

Massey, Douglas S., and Nancy A. Denton. 1993. *American Apartheid: Segregation and the Making of the Underclass*. Cambridge, MA: Harvard Univ. Press.

McIntyre, Alice. 2003. "Through the Eyes of Women: Photovoice and Participatory Research as Tools for Reimagining Place." *Gender, Place, and Culture* 10, no. 1: 47–66.

McKittrick, Katherine. 2006. *Demonic Grounds: Black Women and the Cartographies of Struggle*. Minneapolis: Univ. of Minnesota Press.

McKittrick, Katherine, and Clyde Woods, eds. 2007. *Black Geographies and the Politics of Place*. Toronto/Cambridge, MA: Between the Lines (Canada)/ South End Press (U.S.).

McWilliams, M. 1995. "Struggling for Peace and Justice: Reflections on Women's Activism in Northern Ireland. *Journal of Women's History* 6, no. 4: 13–39.

Melchiorre, G., Y. Pishvazadeh, J. Wechter, and M. Zaritt. 2003. "Southwest Community Center: Department of Parks Recreation and Youth Programs." In *Community Benchmarks Programs*. Syracuse: The Maxwell School of Syracuse Univ.

Miller, Jerome G. 1996. *Search and Destroy: African-American Males in the Criminal Justice System*. New York: Cambridge Univ. Press.

Mills, Charles. 2001. "Black Trash." In *Faces of Environmental Racism*, edited by L. Westra and B. E. Lawson, 73–91. Lanham, MD: Rowman & Littlefield.

Mitchell, Claudia, Naydene DeLange, Relebohile Moletsane, Jean Stuart, and Thabisile Buthelezi. 2005. "Giving a Face to HIV and AIDS: On the Uses of Photovoice by Teachers and Community Health Workers Working with Youth in Rural South Africa." *Qualitative Research in Psychology* 2: 257–70.

Mitchell, Claudia, Relebohile Moletsane, Jean Stuart, Thabisile Buthelezi, and Naydene de Lange. n.d. "Taking Pictures/Taking Action! Visual Methodologies in Working with Young People." *ChildrenFIRST* 9, no. 60: 27–31.

Monk, Carmela. 1989. "15th Ward's Legacy Black Community Lost to '60s Urban Renewal." *The Post-Standard*, February 23, 1989, A1.

Morland, Kimberley, and Steve Wing. 2007. "Food Justice and Health in Communities of Color." In *Growing Smarter: Achieving Livable Communities, Environmental Justice and Regional Equity*, edited by R. D. Bullard, 171–88. Cambridge, MA: MIT Press.

Morland, Kimberley, Steve Wing, Ana Diez Roux, and Charles Poole. 2002. "Neighborhood Characteristics Associated with the Location of Food Stores and Food Service Places." *American Journal of Preventative Medicine* 22, no. 1: 23–39.

Moynihan, Daniel Patrick. 1965. *The Negro Family: The Case for National Action*. Washington, DC: Office of Policy Planning and Research, US Department of Labor.

Mulder, J. T. 2004. "Construction to Start on Home for Mentally Ill; Work on the $3.2 Million, 24-bed Residence in Syracuse Is Set to Begin Monday." *The Post-Standard*, October 23, 2004, Final Edition B5.

Neill, Carly, Beverly D. Leipert, Alicia C. Garcia, and Marita Kloseck. 2011. "Using Photovoice Methodology to Investigate Facilitators and Barriers to Food Acquisition and Preparation by Rural Older Women." *Journal of Nutrition in Gerontology and Geriatrics* 30, no. 3: 225.

Novek, Sheila, Toni Morris-Oswald, and Verena Menec. 2012. "Using Photovoice with Older Adults: Some Methodological Strengths and Issues." *Ageing and Society* 32, no. 3: 451–70.

Nowell, Branda, Shelby L. Berkowitz, Zermarie Deacon, and Pennie Foster-Fishman. 2006. "Revealing the Cues within Community Places: Stories of Identity, History, and Possibility." *American Journal of Community Psychology* 37, nos. 1–2: 29–46.

Park, Robert Ezra, Ernest Watson Burgess, and Roderick Duncan McKenzie. 1967. *The City*. Chicago: Univ. of Chicago Press.

Partnership for Onondaga Creek. 2006. *A Study in Environmental Racism: "New and Significant" Information Regarding Title VI Claim 03R-04-R2*. Syracuse: Partnership for Onondaga Creek.

Phillips, Gayle. 1996. "Stress and Residential Well-being." In *Mental Health in Black America*, edited by H. W. Neighbors and J. S. Jackson. Thousand Oaks, CA: Sage Productions.

Pulido, L. 1996. "A Critical Review of the Methodology of Environmental Racism Research." *Antipode* 28, no. 2: 142–59.

Pulido, Laura. 2000. "Rethinking Environmental Racism: White Privilege and Urban Development in Southern California." *Annals of the Association of American Geographers* 90, no. 1: 12–40.

Pulido, Laura, Steve Sidawi, and Robert O. Vos. 1996. "An Archaeology of Environmental Racism in Los Angeles." *Urban Geography* 17, no. 5: 419–39.

Rofe, Yodan. 2004. "Mapping People's Feelings in a Neighborhood: Technique, Analysis and Applications: Review of Reviewed Item." *Planus—European Journal of Planning Online*. http: //www.planum.net/topics/quality-survey-technique .html.

RoperASW. 2002. "National Geographic—Roper 2002 Global Geographic Literacy Survey." Washington, DC: National Geographic Education Foundation.

Rosen, Daniel, Sara Goodkind, and Mary Lindsey Smith. 2011. "Using Photovoice to Identify Service Needs of Older African American Methadone Clients." *Journal of Social Service Research* 37, no. 5: 526.

Roy, Kevin. 2004. "Three-Block Fathers: Spatial Perceptions and Kin-Work in Low-Income African American Neighborhoods." *Social Problems* 51, no. 4: 528–48.

Rush, Kathy L., Mary Ann Murphy, and Jean Francois Kozak. 2012. "A Photovoice Study of Older Adults' Conceptualizations of Risk." *Journal of Aging Studies* 26, no. 4: 448.

Sacks, Seymour, and Ralph Andrews. 1974. *The Syracuse Black Community, 1970: A Comparative Study.* Syracuse: Univ. College of Syracuse Univ.

Santino, Jack. 2006. "Performative Commemoratives: Spontaneous Shrines and the Public Memorialization of Death." In *Spontaneous Shrines and the Public Memorialization of Death*, edited by Jack Santino, 5–15. New York: Palgrave Macmillan.

Schulz, Amy, David Williams, Barbara Israel, Adam Becker, Edith Parker, Sherman James, and James Jackson. 2000. "Unfair Treatment, Neighborhood Effects and Mental Health in the Detroit Metropolitan Area." *Journal of Health and Social Behavior* 41, no. 3: 314–32.

Sieh, Maureen. 2003. "15th Ward Stood Tall, Fell; 40 Years Ago, a Syracuse Mayor Watched as Urban Renewal Claimed a Neighborhood; Now His Son Is Helping Rebuild It." *The Post-Standard*, September 21, 2003, B1.

———. 2004. "First Project Still Home for Many; Pioneer Homes' Population Has Shifted from Mainly White to Mainly Black." *The Post-Standard*, March 1, 2004, B1.

Simms, Eva-Maria. 2008. "Children's Lived Spaces in the Inner City: Historical and Political Aspects of the Psychology of Place." *The Humanistic Psychologist* 36: 72–89.

Spencer, Michael. 2006. "The Impact of Environmental Justice on Children's Well-being in Detroit Head Start." In *Sparking the Flame: Social Justice & Social Work.* Univ. of Michigan, School of Social Work, Ann Arbor.

Stack, Carol B. 1975. *All Our Kin: Strategies for Survival in a Black Community.* New York: Harper & Row.

Stamps, S. David, and Miriam Burney Stamps. 2008. *Salt City and Its Black Community: A Sociological Study of Syracuse, New York.* Syracuse: Syracuse Univ. Press.

Strack, Robert W., Cathleen Magill, and Kara McDonagh. 2004. "Engaging Youth through Photovoice." *Health Promotion Practice* 5, no. 1: 49–58.

Streng, J. Matt, Scott D. Rhodes, Guadalupe X. Ayala, Eugenia Eng, Ramiro Arceo, and Selena Phipps. 2004. "Realidad Latina: Latino Adolescents, Their School, and a University Use Photovoice to Examine and Address the Influence of Immigration." *Journal of Interprofessional Care* 18, no. 4: 403–15.

Stevens, Christine. 2010. "Lessons from the Field: Using Photovoice with an Ethnically Diverse Population in a HOPE VI Evaluation." *Family and Community Health* 33, no. 4: 275.

Sugrue, Thomas. 1996. *The Origins of the Urban Crisis: Race and Inequality in Postwar Detroit.* Princeton: Princeton University Press.

Syracuse Department of Parks, Recreation and Youth Programs. 2008a. "Kirk Park: City of Syracuse." http:// www.syracuse.ny.us/parks/KirkPark.html.

———. 2008b. "McKinley Park: City of Syracuse." http:// www.syracuse.ny.us /parks/mckinleyPark.html.

———. 2008c. "Onondaga Park: City of Syracuse." http:// www.syracuse.ny.us /parks/onondagaParkUpper.html.

———. 2008d. "Spirit of Jubilee Park: City of Syracuse." http:// www.syracuse .ny.us/parks/spiritOfJubileePark.html.

Szasz, Andrew, and Michael Meuser. 1997. "Environmental Inequalities: Literature Review and Proposals for New Directions in Research and Theory." *Current Sociology* 45, no. 3: 99–120.

Tanjasiri, Sora Park, Rod Lew, Darrah G. Kuratani, Michelle Wong, and Lisa Fu. 2011. "Using Photovoice to Assess and Promote Environmental Approaches to Tobacco Control in AAPI Communities." *Health Promotion Practice* 12, no. 5: 654–65.

Teelucksingh, Cheryl. 2001. "In Somebody's Backyard: Racialized Space and Environmental Justice in Toronto (Canada)." Ph.D. diss., York Univ., Toronto.

———. 2002. "Spatiality and Environmental Justice in Parkdale (Toronto)." *Ethnologies* 24, no. 1: 120–41.

Tyner, James. 2006. *The Geography of Malcolm X: Black Radicalism and the Remaking of American Space.* New York: Routledge.

———. 2007. "Urban Revolutions and the Spaces of Black Radicalism." In *Black Geographies and the Politics of Place*, edited by K. McKittrick and C. Woods, 218–32. Cambridge, MA: South End Press.

van Olphen, Juliana, Amy Schulz, Barbara Israel, Linda Chatters, Laura Klem, Edith Parker, and David Williams. 2003. "Religious Involvement, Social Support, and Health Among African American Women on the East of Detroit." *Journal of General Internal Medicine* 18: 549–57.

Wang, C. 1999. "Photovoice: A Participatory Action Research Strategy Applied to Women's Health." *Journal of Women's Health* 8, no. 2: 185–92.

Wang, Caroline, and Mary Ann Burris. 1994. "Empowerment through Photo Novella: Portraits of Participation." *Health Education Quarterly* 21, no. 2: 171–86.

Wang, Caroline C., Jennifer L. Cash, and Lisa S. Powers. 2000. "Who Knows the Streets as Well as the Homeless? Promoting Personal and Community Action through Photovoice." *Health Promotion Practice* 1, no. 1: 81–89.

Wang, Caroline C., Susan Morrel-Samuels, Peter M. Hutchinson, Lee Bell, and Robert M. Pestronk. 2004. "Flint Photovoice: Community Building among Youths, Adults, and Policymakers." *American Journal of Public Health* 94, no. 6: 911–13.

Wang, Caroline C., and Cheri A Pies. 2004. "Family, Maternal, and Child Health through Photovoice." *Maternal and Child Health Journal* 8, no. 2: 95–102.

Wang, Caroline C., and Yanique A. Redwood-Jones. 2001. "Photovoice Ethics: Perspectives from Flint Photovoice." *Health Education and Behavior* 28, no. 5: 560–72.

Wang, Caroline C., Wu Kun Yi, Zhan Wen Tao, and Kathryn Carovano. 1998. "Photovoice as a Participatory Health Promotion Strategy." *Health Promotion International* 13, no. 1: 75–86.

Washington, O. G. M., and D. Moxley. 2008. "Telling My Story: From Narrative to Exhibit in Illuminating the Lived Experiences of Homelessness among African American Women." *Journal of Health Psychology* 13, no. 2: 154–65.

Watkins, Beverly Xaviera. 2000. "Fantasy, Decay, Abandonment, Defeat and Disease: Community Disintegration in Central Harlem 1960–1990." Ph.D. diss., Columbia Univ., New York.

White, Renee. 2008. "Talking about Sex & HIV: Conceptualizing a New Sociology of Experience." In *Just Methods: Interdisciplinary Feminist Reader*, edited by A. Jagger, 282–90. Newbury Park, CA: Sage.

Williams, Brett. 2001. "A River Runs through Us." *American Anthropologist* 103, no. 2: 409–31.

Wilson, Nance, Meredith Minkler, Stefan Dasho, Nina Wallerstein, and Anna C. Martin. 2006. "Getting to Social Action: The Youth Empowerment Strategies (YES!) Project." *Health Promotion Practice* 7: 1–9.

Woolrych, Richard. 2004. "Empowering Images: Using PhotoVoice with Tenants with Special Needs." *Housing, Care, and Support* 7, no. 1: 31–35.

Wright, Gwendolyn. 1981. *Building the Dream: A Social History of Housing in America.* New York: Pantheon Books.

Zenk, S., A. J. Schulz, B. A. Israel, S. A. James, S. Bao, and M. L. Wilson. 2005. "Neighborhood Racial Composition, Neighborhood Poverty, and Supermarket Accessibility in Metropolitan Detroit." *American Journal of Public Health* 95, no. 4: 660–67.

Index

Page numbers in italics refer to photographs or illustrative material.

"Rethinking Environmental Racism"
    (Pulido), 46
Rich Street, 54, 71
riots. *See* protests and riots
Roesler Park, 52, 53
role models and mentorship, 56, 57, 59,
    61, 70, 73, 100–104
Roosevelt, Franklin D., 28
rootlessnes (anomie), 50
root shock, defined, 35
Roy, Kevin, 102–3

Sacks, Seymour, 36
Saint Vincent DePaul warehouse, 71
Sally's Rape (McCauley), 133
Salvation Army building, 110–11
Santino, Jack, 118
schools, 74. *See also specific school*
Seals, Tom, 67
*Search and Destroy: African-American
    Males in the Criminal Justice System*
    (Miller), 123
sexism, 80, 86, 87, 132
Shintech (Louisiana company), 3
Shirley (participant), 9, 14, 52, 75, 125;
    about, 17–18, 20; comments by,
    65–66, 67, 71, 74–75; mapping proj-
    ect, 57–58; photos taken by, 96, 97,
    98, 104, 106, 111, 112
Shop City, 16, 133
shrines and memorials, 117–19
Schulz, Amy, 78
Simms, Eva-Maria, 49
Sites of Memory (Morrison), 133
situational avoidance, 50–51, 75
sixteenth ward, 40
Snyder, Mitch, 2
social institutions, importance of, 103–11

social justice movements, 128. *See also*
    Black Power movement; civil rights
    movement; environmental justice
    movement
social science, bias and, 5–6
socioeconomic status (SES), 78, 80. *See
    also* class(ism)
South Avenue, 56
South Salina Street, 20–21, 70, 73, 92;
    mapping results, 52, 54, 56, 57, 59
South Side Innovation Center, 73
South Side neighborhood: demograph-
    ics, 13, 121–22; settlement in, 40;
    Syracuse University and, 13, 37–38,
    44, 73, 90. *See also specific location,
    neighborhood, street, or ward*
South Townsend Street, 59
Southwest Community Center, 63–66,
    64, 70, 104; mapping results, 52–53,
    55, 56, 57, 59–60, 63–66
spatiality, 3, 6–10, 130–36; defined, 51;
    place-making, 48, 66; place vulner-
    ability, 66; psychological health and,
    76–81. *See also* racialized space
spontaneous shrines, 118
Stack, Carol, 103
Stamps, Miriam Burney, 40, 42, 43,
    115–17
Stamps, S. David, 40, 42, 43, 115–17
State Street, 36, 37, 38
state violence, 76–77
stereotypes, 76–77
St. Louis (MO), 26
stores, 16, 73
stress. *See* psychological health
studies. *See* reports and studies
suburbanization, 26–27
Supreme Court, U.S., 26
surveillance, 76–77, 90, 134